The
BIBLE
PROMISE
BOOK®

A Treasury of
Christmas
SCRIPTURES

The
BIBLE
PROMISE
BOOK®

A Treasury of
Christmas
SCRIPTURES

BARBOUR BOOKS
An Imprint of Barbour Publishing, Inc.

© 2014 by Barbour Publishing

Written and compiled by JoAnne Simmons.

Print ISBN 978-1-62836-871-0

eBook Editions:
Adobe Digital Edition (.epub) 978-1-63058-590-7
Kindle and MobiPocket Edition (.prc) 978-1-63058-591- 4

All scripture quotations are taken from the King James Version of the Bible.

Published by Barbour Books, an imprint of Barbour Publishing, Inc., P.O. Box 719, Uhrichsville, Ohio 44683, www.barbourbooks.com

Our mission is to publish and distribute inspirational products offering exceptional value and biblical encouragement to the masses.

Printed in the United States of America.

Contents

INTRODUCTION

*T*here's no better time for gifts than the Christmas season! We all have treasured gifts we've received that hold special places in our hearts and holiday memories.

Do you treasure the Bible as a priceless gift? It's our answer for every question. . .our guide for life. It's powerful and everlasting. It's our hope and encouragement. It gives us meaning and purpose. It's God's Word, the very breath of Him. It is a gift that keeps on giving—available and applicable all day, every day, all year long.

The promises of scripture are truths that apply to every season of life. And in the season of Christmas, we can study and apply them in extra-special ways.

This Christmas, amid all the activity, be intentional and faithful to spend time in God's Word. Let this treasury of His promises carry you through both the bustling moments and the calm ones to find the true meaning and joy of the season.

Merry Christmas!

Believe

Believe is a popular word at Christmastime, intended and interpreted in many different ways. But there's only one true thing we can put our faith in during the Christmas season and *every* season of life: our Savior, Jesus Christ, came to earth as a baby—Emmanuel, God with us!—to live and minister, to die for our sins, and to rise again in triumph over death to eternally rescue all who put their trust in Him alone.

And he believed in the LORD; and he counted
it to him for righteousness.

GENESIS 15:6

And the people believed: and when they heard
that the LORD had visited the children of Israel,
and that he had looked upon their affliction,
then they bowed their heads and worshipped.

EXODUS 4:31

And Israel saw that great work which the LORD
did upon the Egyptians: and the people feared
the LORD, and believed the LORD, and his
servant Moses.

EXODUS 14:31

And the LORD said unto Moses, How long will
this people provoke me? and how long will it
be ere they believe me, for all the signs which I
have shewed among them?

NUMBERS 14:11

I had believed to see the goodness of the LORD
in the land of the living. Wait on the LORD: be
of good courage, and he shall strengthen thine
heart: wait, I say, on the LORD.

PSALM 27:13–14

Ye are my witnesses, saith the LORD, and my servant whom I have chosen: that ye may know and believe me, and understand that I am he: before me there was no God formed, neither shall there be after me. I, even I, am the LORD; and beside me there is no saviour.

ISAIAH 43:10–11

And when Jesus was entered into Capernaum, there came unto him a centurion, beseeching him, And saying, Lord, my servant lieth at home sick of the palsy, grievously tormented. And Jesus saith unto him, I will come and heal him. The centurion answered and said, Lord, I am not worthy that thou shouldest come under my roof: but speak the word only, and my servant shall be healed. For I am a man under authority, having soldiers under me: and I say to this man, Go, and he goeth; and to another, Come, and he cometh; and to my servant, Do this, and he doeth it. When Jesus heard it, he marvelled, and said to them that followed, Verily I say unto you, I have not found so great faith, no, not in Israel.

MATTHEW 8:5–10

And Jesus said unto the centurion, Go thy way; and as thou hast believed, so be it done unto thee. And his servant was healed in the selfsame hour.

MATTHEW 8:13

And he entered into a ship, and passed over, and came into his own city. And, behold, they brought to him a man sick of the palsy, lying on a bed: and Jesus seeing their faith said unto the sick of the palsy; Son, be of good cheer; thy sins be forgiven thee.

MATTHEW 9:1–2

And, behold, a woman, which was diseased with an issue of blood twelve years, came behind him, and touched the hem of his garment: For she said within herself, If I may but touch his garment, I shall be whole. But Jesus turned him about, and when he saw her, he said, Daughter, be of good comfort; thy faith hath made thee whole. And the woman was made whole from that hour.

MATTHEW 9:20–22

And when Jesus departed thence, two blind men followed him, crying, and saying, Thou son of David, have mercy on us. And when he was come into the house, the blind men came to him: and Jesus saith unto them, Believe ye that I am able to do this? They said unto him, Yea, Lord. Then touched he their eyes, saying, According to your faith be it unto you. And their eyes were opened.

MATTHEW 9:27–30

If ye have faith as a grain of mustard seed, ye shall say unto this mountain, Remove hence to yonder place; and it shall remove; and nothing shall be impossible unto you.

MATTHEW 17:20

And whoso shall receive one such little child in my name receiveth me. But whoso shall offend one of these little ones which believe in me, it were better for him that a millstone were hanged about his neck, and that he were drowned in the depth of the sea.

MATTHEW 18:5–6

And when he saw a fig tree in the way, he came
to it, and found nothing thereon, but leaves
only, and said unto it, Let no fruit grow on thee
henceforward for ever. And presently the fig tree
withered away. And when the disciples saw it,
they marvelled, saying, How soon is the fig tree
withered away! Jesus answered and said unto
them, Verily I say unto you, If ye have faith, and
doubt not, ye shall not only do this which is done
to the fig tree, but also if ye shall say unto this
mountain, Be thou removed, and be thou cast into
the sea; it shall be done. And all things, whatsoever
ye shall ask in prayer, believing, ye shall receive.

MATTHEW 21:19–22

Now after that John was put in prison, Jesus
came into Galilee, preaching the gospel of
the kingdom of God, And saying, The time is
fulfilled, and the kingdom of God is at hand:
repent ye, and believe the gospel.

MARK 1:14–15

But the woman fearing and trembling, knowing
what was done in her, came and fell down before
him, and told him all the truth. And he said unto
her, Daughter, thy faith hath made thee whole;
go in peace, and be whole of thy plague.

MARK 5:33–34

And again he entered into Capernaum after some days; and it was noised that he was in the house. And straightway many were gathered together, insomuch that there was no room to receive them, no, not so much as about the door: and he preached the word unto them. And they come unto him, bringing one sick of the palsy, which was borne of four. And when they could not come nigh unto him for the press, they uncovered the roof where he was: and when they had broken it up, they let down the bed wherein the sick of the palsy lay. When Jesus saw their faith, he said unto the sick of the palsy, Son, thy sins be forgiven thee.

MARK 2:1–5

As soon as Jesus heard the word that was spoken, he saith unto the ruler of the synagogue, Be not afraid, only believe.

MARK 5:36

Jesus said unto him, If thou canst believe, all things are possible to him that believeth. And straightway the father of the child cried out, and said with tears, Lord, I believe; help thou mine unbelief.

MARK 9:23–24

And Jesus answered and said unto him, What wilt thou that I should do unto thee? The blind man said unto him, Lord, that I might receive my sight. And Jesus said unto him, Go thy way; thy faith hath made thee whole. And immediately he received his sight, and followed Jesus in the way.

MARK 10:51–52

And Jesus answering saith unto them, Have faith in God. For verily I say unto you, That whosoever shall say unto this mountain, Be thou removed, and be thou cast into the sea; and shall not doubt in his heart, but shall believe that those things which he saith shall come to pass; he shall have whatsoever he saith. Therefore I say unto you, What things soever ye desire, when ye pray, believe that ye receive them, and ye shall have them.

MARK 11:22–24

And blessed is she that believed: for there shall be a performance of those things which were told her from the Lord.

LUKE 1:45

And he said unto them, Go ye into all the
world, and preach the gospel to every creature.
He that believeth and is baptized shall be saved;
but he that believeth not shall be damned.

MARK 16:15–16

While he yet spake, there cometh one from the
ruler of the synagogue's house, saying to him,
Thy daughter is dead; trouble not the Master.
But when Jesus heard it, he answered him,
saying, Fear not: believe only, and she shall be
made whole.

LUKE 8:49–50

And the apostles said unto the Lord,
Increase our faith. And the Lord said,
If ye had faith as a grain of mustard
seed, ye might say unto this sycamine
tree, Be thou plucked up by the root,
and be thou planted in the sea;
and it should obey you.

LUKE 17:5–6

And Jesus said unto him, Receive thy sight: thy
faith hath saved thee.

LUKE 18:42

He came unto his own, and his own received him not. But as many as received him, to them gave he power to become the sons of God, even to them that believe on his name.

JOHN 1:11–12

Nathanael answered and saith unto him, Rabbi, thou art the Son of God; thou art the King of Israel. Jesus answered and said unto him, Because I said unto thee, I saw thee under the fig tree, believest thou? thou shalt see greater things than these. And he saith unto him, Verily, verily, I say unto you, Hereafter ye shall see heaven open, and the angels of God ascending and descending upon the Son of man.

JOHN 1:49–51

This beginning of miracles did Jesus in Cana of Galilee, and manifested forth his glory; and his disciples believed on him.

JOHN 2:11

Jesus answered and said unto them, Destroy this temple, and in three days I will raise it up. Then said the Jews, Forty and six years was this temple in building, and wilt thou rear it up in three days? But he spake of the temple of his body. When therefore he was risen from the dead, his disciples remembered that he had said this unto them; and they believed the scripture, and the word which Jesus had said. Now when he was in Jerusalem at the passover, in the feast day, many believed in his name, when they saw the miracles which he did.

JOHN 2:19–23

For God so loved the world,
that he gave his only begotten Son,
that whosoever believeth in him should
not perish, but have everlasting life.
JOHN 3:16

He that believeth on the Son hath
everlasting life: and he that believeth
not the Son shall not see life; but the
wrath of God abideth on him.

JOHN 3:36

And many of the Samaritans of that city
believed on him for the saying of the woman,
which testified, He told me all that ever I did.
So when the Samaritans were come unto him,
they besought him that he would tarry with
them: and he abode there two days. And many
more believed because of his own word; And
said unto the woman, Now we believe, not
because of thy saying: for we have heard him
ourselves, and know that this is indeed the
Christ, the Saviour of the world.

JOHN 4:39–42

The nobleman saith unto him,
Sir, come down ere my child die.
Jesus saith unto him, Go thy way;
thy son liveth. And the man believed
the word that Jesus had spoken unto
him, and he went his way. And as he
was now going down, his servants met
him, and told him, saying, Thy son
liveth Then enquired he of them the
hour when he began to amend.
And they said unto him, Yesterday at
the seventh hour the fever left him.
So the father knew that it was at the
same hour, in the which Jesus said
unto him, Thy son liveth: and himself
believed, and his whole house.

JOHN 4:49–53

Then Simon Peter answered him, Lord, to
whom shall we go? thou hast the words of
eternal life. And we believe and are sure that
thou art that Christ, the Son of the living God.

JOHN 6:68–69

Let not your heart be troubled:
ye believe in God, believe also in me.
In my Father's house are many
mansions: if it were not so, I would
have told you. I go to prepare a place
for you. And if I go and prepare a place
for you, I will come again, and receive
you unto myself; that where I am,
there ye may be also.

John 14:1–3

Jesus heard that they had cast him out; and
when he had found him, he said unto him, Dost
thou believe on the Son of God? He answered
and said, Who is he, Lord, that I might believe
on him? And Jesus said unto him, Thou hast
both seen him, and it is he that talketh with
thee. And he said, Lord, I believe. And he
worshipped him.

John 9:35–38

Jesus saith unto him, Have I been so long time with you, and yet hast thou not known me, Philip? he that hath seen me hath seen the Father; and how sayest thou then, Show us the Father? Believest thou not that I am in the Father, and the Father in me? the words that I speak unto you I speak not of myself: but the Father that dwelleth in me, he doeth the works. Believe me that I am in the Father, and the Father in me: or else believe me for the very works' sake. Verily, verily, I say unto you, He that believeth on me, the works that I do shall he do also; and greater works than these shall he do; because I go unto my Father. And whatsoever ye shall ask in my name, that will I do, that the Father may be glorified in the Son. If ye shall ask any thing in my name, I will do it.

JOHN 14:9–14

*Ye have heard how I said unto you,
I go away, and come again unto you.
If ye loved me, ye would rejoice,
because I said, I go unto the Father:
for my Father is greater than I.
And now I have told you before it
come to pass, that, when it is come
to pass, ye might believe.*

JOHN 14:28–29

For the Father himself loveth you, because ye have loved me, and have believed that I came out from God.

JOHN 16:27

Jesus saith unto him, Thomas, because thou hast seen me, thou hast believed: blessed are they that have not seen, and yet have believed. And many other signs truly did Jesus in the presence of his disciples, which are not written in this book: But these are written, that ye might believe that Jesus is the Christ, the Son of God; and that believing ye might have life through his name.

JOHN 20:29–31

And Stephen, full of faith and power, did great wonders and miracles among the people.
ACTS 6:8

And Philip said, If thou believest with all thine heart, thou mayest. And he answered and said, I believe that Jesus Christ is the Son of God.

ACTS 8:37

*Be it known unto you therefore, men
and brethren, that through this man is
preached unto you the forgiveness of sins:
And by him all that believe are justified
from all things, from which ye could not
be justified by the law of Moses.*

Acts 13:38–39

And when they had preached the gospel to
that city, and had taught many, they returned
again to Lystra, and to Iconium, and Antioch,
Confirming the souls of the disciples, and
exhorting them to continue in the faith, and
that we must through much tribulation enter
into the kingdom of God.

Acts 14:21–22

And when there had been much disputing, Peter
rose up, and said unto them, Men and brethren,
ye know how that a good while ago God made
choice among us, that the Gentiles by my mouth
should hear the word of the gospel, and believe.
And God, which knoweth the hearts, bare them
witness, giving them the Holy Ghost, even as he
did unto us; And put no difference between us
and them, purifying their hearts by faith.

Acts 15:7–9

*But we believe that through
the grace of the Lord Jesus Christ
we shall be saved, even as they.*

Acts 15:11

And the keeper of the prison awaking out of his
sleep, and seeing the prison doors open, he drew
out his sword, and would have killed himself,
supposing that the prisoners had been fled. But
Paul cried with a loud voice, saying, Do thyself
no harm: for we are all here. Then he called for
a light, and sprang in, and came trembling, and
fell down before Paul and Silas, And brought
them out, and said, Sirs, what must I do to be
saved? And they said, Believe on the Lord Jesus
Christ, and thou shalt be saved, and thy house.
And they spake unto him the word of the Lord,
and to all that were in his house. And he took
them the same hour of the night, and washed
their stripes; and was baptized, he and all his,
straightway. And when he had brought them
into his house, he set meat before them, and
rejoiced, believing in God with all his house.

Acts 16:27–34

For there stood by me this night the angel of God, whose I am, and whom I serve, Saying, Fear not, Paul; thou must be brought before Caesar: and, lo, God hath given thee all them that sail with thee. Wherefore, sirs, be of good cheer: for I believe God, that it shall be even as it was told me.

ACTS 27:23–25

First, I thank my God through Jesus Christ for you all, that your faith is spoken of throughout the whole world.
ROMANS 1:8

For I am not ashamed of the gospel of Christ: for it is the power of God unto salvation to every one that believeth; to the Jew first, and also to the Greek. For therein is the righteousness of God revealed from faith to faith: as it is written, The just shall live by faith.
ROMANS 1:16–17

What advantage then hath the Jew?
or what profit is there of circumcision?
Much every way: chiefly, because that
unto them were committed the oracles
of God. For what if some did not
believe? shall their unbelief make the
faith of God without effect? God forbid:
yea, let God be true, but every man a
liar; as it is written, That thou mightest
be justified in thy sayings, and mightest
overcome when thou art judged.

ROMANS 3:1–4

Even the righteousness of God which is by faith
of Jesus Christ unto all and upon all them that
believe: for there is no difference: For all have
sinned, and come short of the glory of God;
Being justified freely by his grace through the
redemption that is in Christ Jesus: Whom God
hath set forth to be a propitiation through faith
in his blood, to declare his righteousness for
the remission of sins that are past, through the
forbearance of God; To declare, I say, at this
time his righteousness: that he might be just,
and the justifier of him which believeth in Jesus.

ROMANS 3:22–26

But to him that worketh not, but believeth
on him that justifieth the ungodly, his faith is
counted for righteousness.

Romans 4:5

And being not weak in faith, he considered not
his own body now dead, when he was about an
hundred years old, neither yet the deadness of
Sarah's womb: He staggered not at the promise
of God through unbelief; but was strong in
faith, giving glory to God; And being fully
persuaded that, what he had promised, he was
able also to perform.

Romans 4:19–21

Therefore being justified by faith, we have peace
with God through our Lord Jesus Christ: By
whom also we have access by faith into this
grace wherein we stand, and rejoice in hope of
the glory of God.

Romans 5:1–2

That if thou shalt confess with thy mouth the
Lord Jesus, and shalt believe in thine heart that
God hath raised him from the dead, thou shalt
be saved. For with the heart man believeth unto
righteousness; and with the mouth confession is
made unto salvation.

Romans 10:9–10

For whosoever shall call upon the name of the Lord shall be saved. How then shall they call on him in whom they have not believed? and how shall they believe in him of whom they have not heard? and how shall they hear without a preacher? And how shall they preach, except they be sent? as it is written, How beautiful are the feet of them that preach the gospel of peace, and bring glad tidings of good things!

ROMANS 10:13–15

So then faith cometh by hearing, and hearing by the word of God.
ROMANS 10:17

Therefore we are always confident, knowing that, whilst we are at home in the body, we are absent from the Lord: (For we walk by faith, not by sight.)

2 CORINTHIANS 5:6–7

Knowing that a man is not justified by the works of the law, but by the faith of Jesus Christ, even we have believed in Jesus Christ, that we might be justified by the faith of Christ, and not by the works of the law: for by the works of the law shall no flesh be justified.

GALATIANS 2:16

I am crucified with Christ: nevertheless I live; yet not I, but Christ liveth in me: and the life which I now live in the flesh I live by the faith of the Son of God, who loved me, and gave himself for me.

For ye are all the children of God by faith in Christ Jesus.

GALATIANS 3:26

The eyes of your understanding being enlightened; that ye may know what is the hope of his calling, and what the riches of the glory of his inheritance in the saints, And what is the exceeding greatness of his power to us-ward who believe, according to the working of his mighty power.

EPHESIANS 1:18–19

For this cause also thank we God without ceasing, because, when ye received the word of God which ye heard of us, ye received it not as the word of men, but as it is in truth, the word of God, which effectually worketh also in you that believe.

1 THESSALONIANS 2:13

For if we believe that Jesus died and rose again, even so them also which sleep in Jesus will God bring with him.

1 THESSALONIANS 4:14

This is a faithful saying and worthy of all acceptation. For therefore we both labour and suffer reproach, because we trust in the living God, who is the Saviour of all men, specially of those that believe.

1 TIMOTHY 4:9–10

But continue thou in the things which thou hast learned and hast been assured of, knowing of whom thou hast learned them; And that from a child thou hast known the holy scriptures, which are able to make thee wise unto salvation through faith which is in Christ Jesus. All scripture is given by inspiration of God, and is profitable for doctrine, for reproof, for correction, for instruction in righteousness: That the man of God may be perfect, thoroughly furnished unto all good works.

2 TIMOTHY 3:14–17

For I am now ready to be offered, and the time of my departure is at hand. I have fought a good fight, I have finished my course, I have kept the faith: Henceforth there is laid up for me a crown of righteousness, which the Lord, the righteous judge, shall give me at that day: and not to me only, but unto all them also that love his appearing.

2 TIMOTHY 4:6–8

Now faith is the substance
of things hoped for,
the evidence of things not seen.
HEBREWS 11:1

But without faith it is impossible to please him: for he that cometh to God must believe that he is, and that he is a rewarder of them that diligently seek him.

HEBREWS 11:6

What doth it profit, my brethren,
though a man say he hath faith,
and have not works? can faith save
him? If a brother or sister be naked,
and destitute of daily food, And one
of you say unto them, Depart in
peace, be ye warmed and filled;
notwithstanding ye give them not those
things which are needful to the body;
what doth it profit? Even so faith,
if it hath not works, is dead, being
alone. Yea, a man may say, Thou hast
faith, and I have works: shew me thy
faith without thy works, and I will
shew thee my faith by my works. Thou
believest that there is one God; thou
doest well: the devils also believe, and
tremble. But wilt thou know, O vain
man, that faith without works is dead?

JAMES 2:14–20

And this is his commandment, That we should
believe on the name of his Son Jesus Christ, and
love one another, as he gave us commandment.

1 JOHN 3:23

The trying of your faith worketh patience.

JAMES 1:3

Beloved, believe not every spirit, but try the spirits whether they are of God: because many false prophets are gone out into the world. Hereby know ye the Spirit of God: Every spirit that confesseth that Jesus Christ is come in the flesh is of God: And every spirit that confesseth not that Jesus Christ is come in the flesh is not of God: and this is that spirit of antichrist, whereof ye have heard that it should come; and even now already is it in the world.

1 JOHN 4:1–3

He that believeth on the Son of God hath the witness in himself: he that believeth not God hath made him a liar; because he believeth not the record that God gave of his Son. And this is the record, that God hath given to us eternal life, and this life is in his Son. He that hath the Son hath life; and he that hath not the Son of God hath not life.

1 JOHN 5:10–12

Blessings

Receiving gifts is a part of the joy and fun of the Christmas season, but no better gifts exist than those given by our heavenly Father. His blessings here on earth—and His blessings yet to come—are described in the promises of His Word. Open your eyes, your hands, your heart, and receive them!

And it shall come to pass, if thou shalt hearken diligently unto the voice of the LORD thy God, to observe and to do all his commandments which I command thee this day, that the LORD thy God will set thee on high above all nations of the earth: And all these blessings shall come on thee, and overtake thee, if thou shalt hearken unto the voice of the LORD thy God. Blessed shalt thou be in the city, and blessed shalt thou be in the field.

DEUTERONOMY 28:1–3

The Lord shall command the blessing upon thee in thy storehouses, and in all that thou settest thine hand unto; and he shall bless thee in the land which the Lord thy God giveth thee. The Lord shall establish thee an holy people unto himself, as he hath sworn unto thee, if thou shalt keep the commandments of the Lord thy God, and walk in his ways.

DEUTERONOMY 28:8–9

Salvation belongeth unto the LORD: thy blessing is upon thy people.

PSALM 3:8

Who shall ascend into the hill of the LORD?
or who shall stand in his holy place? He that
hath clean hands, and a pure heart; who hath
not lifted up his soul unto vanity, nor sworn
deceitfully. He shall receive the blessing from
the LORD, and righteousness from the God of
his salvation.

PSALM 24:3–5

The blessing of the LORD, it maketh rich, and
he addeth no sorrow with it.

PROVERBS 10:22

He that saith unto the wicked, Thou are
righteous; him shall the people curse, nations
shall abhor him: But to them that rebuke him
shall be delight, and a good blessing shall come
upon them.

PROVERBS 24:24–25

A faithful man shall abound with blessings: but he
that maketh haste to be rich shall not be innocent.

PROVERBS 28:20

And I will make them and the places round
about my hill a blessing; and I will cause the
shower to come down in his season; there shall
be showers of blessing.

EZEKIEL 34:26

Behold that which I have seen: it is good and comely for one to eat and to drink, and to enjoy the good of all his labour that he taketh under the sun all the days of his life, which God giveth him: for it is his portion. Every man also to whom God hath given riches and wealth, and hath given him power to eat thereof, and to take his portion, and to rejoice in his labour; this is the gift of God. For he shall not much remember the days of his life; because God answereth him in the joy of his heart.

ECCLESIASTES 5:18–20

Yet now hear, O Jacob my servant; and Israel, whom I have chosen: Thus saith the Lord that made thee, and formed thee from the womb, which will help thee; Fear not, O Jacob, my servant; and thou, Jesurun, whom I have chosen. For I will pour water upon him that is thirsty, and floods upon the dry ground: I will pour my spirit upon thy seed, and my blessing upon thine offspring.

ISAIAH 44:1–3

Bring ye all the tithes into the storehouse, that there may be meat in mine house, and prove me now herewith, saith the Lord of hosts, if I will not open you the windows of heaven, and pour you out a blessing, that there shall not be room enough to receive it.

MALACHI 3:10

But seek ye first the kingdom of God, and his righteousness; and all these things shall be added unto you.

MATTHEW 6:33

Or what man is there of you, whom if his son ask bread, will he give him a stone? Or if he ask a fish, will he give him a serpent? If ye then, being evil, know how to give good gifts unto your children, how much more shall your Father which is in heaven give good things to them that ask him?

MATTHEW 7:9–11

And blessed is she that believed: for there shall be a performance of those things which were told her from the Lord.

LUKE 1:45

*Jesus answered and said unto her,
If thou knewest the gift of God,
and who it is that saith to thee, Give
me to drink; thou wouldest have asked
of him, and he would have given thee
living water. The woman saith unto
him, Sir, thou hast nothing to draw
with, and the well is deep: from whence
then hast thou that living water?
Art thou greater than our father Jacob,
which gave us the well, and drank
thereof himself, and his children,
and his cattle? Jesus answered and said
unto her, Whosoever drinketh of this
water shall thirst again: But whosoever
drinketh of the water that I shall give
him shall never thirst; but the water
that I shall give him shall be in him
a well of water springing up into
everlasting life.*

JOHN 4:10–14

For as we have many members in one body, and all members have not the same office: So we, being many, are one body in Christ, and every one members one of another. Having then gifts differing according to the grace that is given to us, whether prophecy, let us prophesy according to the proportion of faith; Or ministry, let us wait on our ministering: or he that teacheth, on teaching; Or he that exhorteth, on exhortation: he that giveth, let him do it with simplicity; he that ruleth, with diligence; he that sheweth mercy, with cheerfulness.

ROMANS 12:4–8

And God is able to make all grace abound toward you; that ye, always having all sufficiency in all things, may abound to every good work.

2 CORINTHIANS 9:8

Blessed be the God and Father of our Lord Jesus Christ, who hath blessed us with all spiritual blessings in heavenly places in Christ.

EPHESIANS 1:3

How shall we escape, if we neglect so great salvation; which at the first began to be spoken by the Lord, and was confirmed unto us by them that heard him; God also bearing them witness, both with signs and wonders, and with divers miracles, and gifts of the Holy Ghost, according to his own will?

HEBREWS 2:3–4

For the earth which drinketh in the rain that cometh oft upon it, and bringeth forth herbs meet for them by whom it is dressed, receiveth blessing from God.

HEBREWS 6:7

For when God made promise to Abraham, because he could swear by no greater, he sware by himself, Saying, Surely blessing I will bless thee, and multiplying I will multiply thee.

HEBREWS 6:13–14

If any of you lack wisdom, let him ask of God, that giveth to all men liberally, and upbraideth not; and it shall be given him.

JAMES 1:5

Children

Many songs and sayings agree that "Christmas is for children." And the most excitement for the season is surely displayed by little ones. God's Word talks about children in a very special way. . .and Jesus came to us at Christmas as a tiny babe! In God's promises regarding children, there are profound lessons for people of every age to learn.

And he lifted up his eyes, and saw the women and the children; and said, Who are those with thee? And he said, The children which God hath graciously given thy servant.

GENESIS 33:5

For this child I prayed; and the LORD hath given me my petition which I asked of him: Therefore also I have lent him to the LORD; as long as he liveth he shall be lent to the LORD. And he worshipped the LORD there.

1 SAMUEL 1:27–28

He maketh the barren woman to keep house, and to be a joyful mother of children. Praise ye the Lord.

PSALM 113:9

Lo, children are an heritage of the LORD: and the fruit of the womb is his reward. As arrows are in the hand of a mighty man; so are children of the youth. Happy is the man that hath his quiver full of them: they shall not be ashamed, but they shall speak with the enemies in the gate.

PSALM 127:3–5

Children's children are the crown of old men;
and the glory of children are their fathers.

PROVERBS 17:6

For thou hast possessed my reins: thou hast
covered me in my mother's womb. I will praise
thee; for I am fearfully and wonderfully made:
marvellous are thy works; and that my soul
knoweth right well. My substance was not
hid from thee, when I was made in secret, and
curiously wrought in the lowest parts of the
earth. Thine eyes did see my substance, yet being
unperfect; and in thy book all my members were
written, which in continuance were fashioned,
when as yet there was none of them.

PSALM 139:13–16

The just man walketh in his integrity: his
children are blessed after him.

PROVERBS 20:7

Train up a child in the way he should go: and
when he is old, he will not depart from it.

PROVERBS 22:6

The rod and reproof give wisdom: but a child
left to himself bringeth his mother to shame.

PROVERBS 29:15

Before I formed thee in the belly I knew thee; and before thou camest forth out of the womb I sanctified thee, and I ordained thee a prophet unto the nations.

JEREMIAH 1:5

At the same time came the disciples unto Jesus, saying, Who is the greatest in the kingdom of heaven? And Jesus called a little child unto him, and set him in the midst of them, And said, Verily I say unto you, Except ye be converted, and become as little children, ye shall not enter into the kingdom of heaven. Whosoever therefore shall humble himself as this little child, the same is greatest in the kingdom of heaven. And whoso shall receive one such little child in my name receiveth me. But whoso shall offend one of these little ones which believe in me, it were better for him that a millstone were hanged about his neck, and that he were drowned in the depth of the sea.

MATTHEW 18:1–6

Take heed that ye despise not one of these little ones; for I say unto you, That in heaven their angels do always behold the face of my Father which is in heaven.

MATTHEW 18:10

And he sat down, and called the twelve, and saith unto them, If any man desire to be first, the same shall be last of all, and servant of all. And he took a child, and set him in the midst of them: and when he had taken him in his arms, he said unto them, Whosoever shall receive one of such children in my name, receiveth me: and whosoever shall receive me, receiveth not me, but him that sent me.

MARK 9:35–37

And they brought young children to him, that he should touch them: and his disciples rebuked those that brought them. But when Jesus saw it, he was much displeased, and said unto them, Suffer the little children to come unto me, and forbid them not: for of such is the kingdom of God. Verily I say unto you, Whosoever shall not receive the kingdom of God as a little child, he shall not enter therein. And he took them up in his arms, put his hands upon them, and blessed them.

MARK 10:13–16

*In that hour Jesus rejoiced in spirit,
and said, I thank thee, O Father,
Lord of heaven and earth, that thou
hast hid these things from the wise
and prudent, and hast revealed them
unto babes: even so, Father; for so it
seemed good in thy sight.*

LUKE 10:21

And they brought unto him also infants, that
he would touch them: but when his disciples
saw it, they rebuked them. But Jesus called them
unto him, and said, Suffer little children to
come unto me, and forbid them not: for of such
is the kingdom of God. Verily I say unto you,
Whosoever shall not receive the kingdom of
God as a little child shall in no wise enter therein.

LUKE 18:15–17

A woman when she is in travail hath sorrow,
because her hour is come: but as soon as she
is delivered of the child, she remembereth no
more the anguish, for joy that a man is born
into the world.

JOHN 16:21

Provoke not your children to wrath: but bring
them up in the nurture and admonition of the
Lord.

EPHESIANS 6:4

Compassion

For many people, the Christmas season is a tough time due to loss of loved ones, the stress and pain of broken or troubled relationships, financial strife. . .the list goes on and on. There are so many heartaches in this fallen world. But God knows and cares about each and every one. He comforts us in all our troubles through the promises in His Word. As we receive His compassion, we, in turn, can extend it to others.

Thus speaketh the Lord of hosts,
saying, Execute true judgment,
and shew mercy and compassions
every man to his brother: And oppress
not the widow, nor the fatherless,
the stranger, nor the poor; and let
none of you imagine evil against
his brother in your heart.
ZECHARIAH 7:9–10

For if ye forgive men their trespasses, your
heavenly Father will also forgive you: But if ye
forgive not men their trespasses, neither will
your Father forgive your trespasses.

MATTHEW 6:14–15

Are not two sparrows sold for a farthing?
and one of them shall not fall on the ground
without your Father. But the very hairs of your
head are all numbered. Fear ye not therefore, ye
are of more value than many sparrows.

MATTHEW 10:29–31

And Jesus went forth, and saw a great
multitude, and was moved with compassion
toward them, and he healed their sick.

MATTHEW 14:14

Grace be to you and peace from God our Father, and from the Lord Jesus Christ. Blessed be God, even the Father of our Lord Jesus Christ, the Father of mercies, and the God of all comfort; Who comforteth us in all our tribulation, that we may be able to comfort them which are in any trouble, by the comfort wherewith we ourselves are comforted of God. For as the sufferings of Christ abound in us, so our consolation also aboundeth by Christ. And whether we be afflicted, it is for your consolation and salvation, which is effectual in the enduring of the same sufferings which we also suffer: or whether we be comforted, it is for your consolation and salvation. And our hope of you is stedfast, knowing, that as ye are partakers of the sufferings, so shall ye be also of the consolation.

2 CORINTHIANS 1:2–7

Bear ye one another's burdens,
and so fulfil the law of Christ.
GALATIANS 6:2

Let all bitterness, and wrath, and anger, and clamour, and evil speaking, be put away from you, with all malice: And be ye kind one to another, tenderhearted, forgiving one another, even as God for Christ's sake hath forgiven you.

EPHESIANS 4:31–32

If there be therefore any consolation in Christ, if any comfort of love, if any fellowship of the Spirit, if any bowels and mercies, Fulfil ye my joy, that ye be likeminded, having the same love, being of one accord, of one mind. Let nothing be done through strife or vainglory; but in lowliness of mind let each esteem other better than themselves. Look not every man on his own things, but every man also on the things of others.

PHILIPPIANS 2:1–4

Put on therefore, as the elect of God, holy and beloved, bowels of mercies, kindness, humbleness of mind, meekness, longsuffering; Forbearing one another, and forgiving one another, if any man have a quarrel against any: even as Christ forgave you, so also do ye. And above all these things put on charity, which is the bond of perfectness.

COLOSSIANS 3:12–14

*Pure religion and undefiled
before God and the Father is this,
To visit the fatherless and widows in
their affliction, and to keep himself
unspotted from the world.*

JAMES 1:27

Family and Friends

The Christmas season is a time to gather with family and friends, sometimes traveling great distances just to be together. God is the Creator of human relationships. He knows it is not good for us to be alone. The promises in His Word regarding friends and family guide us in love and fellowship with one another.

And God said, Let us make man in our image, after our likeness: and let them have dominion over the fish of the sea, and over the fowl of the air, and over the cattle, and over all the earth, and over every creeping thing that creepeth upon the earth.
So God created man in his own image, in the image of God created he him; male and female created he them.
And God blessed them, and God said unto them, Be fruitful, and multiply, and replenish the earth, and subdue it: and have dominion over the fish of the sea, and over the fowl of the air, and over every living thing that moveth upon the earth.

GENESIS 1:26–28

And the LORD God said, It is not good that the man should be alone; I will make him an help meet for him.

GENESIS 2:18

And the LORD God caused a deep sleep to fall upon Adam, and he slept: and he took one of his ribs, and closed up the flesh instead thereof; And the rib, which the LORD God had taken from man, made he a woman, and brought her unto the man. And Adam said, This is now bone of my bones, and flesh of my flesh: she shall be called Woman, because she was taken out of Man. Therefore shall a man leave his father and his mother, and shall cleave unto his wife: and they shall be one flesh. And they were both naked, the man and his wife, and were not ashamed.

GENESIS 2:21–25

And Adam called his wife's name Eve; because she was the mother of all living.

GENESIS 3:20

Honour thy father and thy mother: that thy days may be long upon the land which the Lord thy God giveth thee.

EXODUS 20:12

Ye shall fear every man his mother, and his father.

LEVITICUS 19:3

Hear, O Israel: The LORD our God is one LORD: And thou shalt love the LORD thy God with all thine heart, and with all thy soul, and with all thy might. And these words, which I command thee this day, shall be in thine heart: And thou shalt teach them diligently unto thy children, and shalt talk of them when thou sittest in thine house, and when thou walkest by the way, and when thou liest down, and when thou risest up. And thou shalt bind them for a sign upon thine hand, and they shall be as frontlets between thine eyes. And thou shalt write them upon the posts of thy house, and on thy gates.

DEUTERONOMY 6:4–9

Observe and hear all these words which I command thee, that it may go well with thee, and with thy children after thee for ever, when thou doest that which is good and right in the sight of the Lord thy God.

DEUTERONOMY 12:28

And it came to pass, when he had made an end of speaking unto Saul, that the soul of Jonathan was knit with the soul of David, and Jonathan loved him as his own soul. And Saul took him that day, and would let him go no more home to his father's house. Then Jonathan and David made a covenant, because he loved him as his own soul.

1 SAMUEL 18:1–3

But the mercy of the LORD is from everlasting to everlasting upon them that fear him, and his righteousness unto children's children.

PSALM 103:17

Hear, ye children, the instruction of a father, and attend to know understanding. For I give you good doctrine, forsake ye not my law. For I was my father's son, tender and only beloved in the sight of my mother.

PROVERBS 4:1–3

My son, keep thy father's commandment, and forsake not the law of thy mother: Bind them continually upon thine heart, and tie them about thy neck. When thou goest, it shall lead thee; when thou sleepest, it shall keep thee; and when thou awakest, it shall talk with thee.

PROVERBS 6:20–22

A wise son maketh a glad father: but a foolish son is the heaviness of his mother.

PROVERBS 10:1

A virtuous woman is a crown to her husband: but she that maketh ashamed is as rottenness in his bones.

PROVERBS 12:4

A wise son heareth his father's instruction: but a scorner heareth not rebuke.

PROVERBS 13:1

He that walketh with wise men shall be wise: but a companion of fools shall be destroyed.

PROVERBS 13:20

A good man leaveth an inheritance to his children's children.

PROVERBS 13:22

Every wise woman buildeth her house: but the foolish plucketh it down with her hands.

PROVERBS 14:1

A brother offended is harder to be won than a strong city: and their contentions are like the bars of a castle.

PROVERBS 18:19

A man that hath friends must shew himself friendly: and there is a friend that sticketh closer than a brother.

PROVERBS 18:24

It is better to dwell in the wilderness, than with a contentious and an angry woman.

PROVERBS 21:19

Hearken unto thy father that begat thee, and despise not thy mother when she is old.

PROVERBS 23:22

The father of the righteous shall greatly rejoice: and he that begetteth a wise child shall have joy of him. Thy father and thy mother shall be glad, and she that bare thee shall rejoice.

PROVERBS 23:24–25

*Iron sharpeneth iron; so a man
sharpeneth the countenance of his friend.*
PROVERBS 27:17

Two are better than one; because they have a
good reward for their labour. For if they fall, the
one will lift up his fellow: but woe to him that is
alone when he falleth; for he hath not another to
help him up. Again, if two lie together, then they
have heat: but how can one be warm alone? And
if one prevail against him, two shall withstand
him; and a threefold cord is not quickly broken.
ECCLESIASTES 4:9–12

And all thy children shall be taught of the
LORD; and great shall be the peace of thy
children. In righteousness shalt thou be
established: thou shalt be far from oppression;
for thou shalt not fear: and from terror; for it
shall not come near thee.
ISAIAH 54:13–14

Behold, I will send you Elijah the prophet
before the coming of the great and dreadful day
of the LORD: And he shall turn the heart of
the fathers to the children, and the heart of the
children to their fathers, lest I come and smite
the earth with a curse.
MALACHI 4:5–6

Again I say unto you, That if two of you shall agree on earth as touching any thing that they shall ask, it shall be done for them of my Father which is in heaven. For where two or three are gathered together in my name, there am I in the midst of them.

MATTHEW 18:19–20

Then came Peter to him, and said, Lord, how oft shall my brother sin against me, and I forgive him? till seven times? Jesus saith unto him, I say not unto thee, Until seven times: but, Until seventy times seven.

MATTHEW 18:21–22

This is my commandment, That ye love one another, as I have loved you. Greater love hath no man than this, that a man lay down his life for his friends.

JOHN 15:12–13

Henceforth I call you not servants; for the servant knoweth not what his lord doeth: but I have called you friends; for all things that I have heard of my Father I have made known unto you.

JOHN 15:15

Then Peter said unto them, Repent, and be baptized every one of you in the name of Jesus Christ for the remission of sins, and ye shall receive the gift of the Holy Ghost. For the promise is unto you, and to your children, and to all that are afar off, even as many as the LORD our God shall call.

ACTS 2:38–39

Be kindly affectioned one to another with brotherly love; in honour preferring one another.
ROMANS 12:10

But I would have you know, that the head of every man is Christ; and the head of the woman is the man; and the head of Christ is God.
1 CORINTHIANS 11:3

For this cause I bow my knees unto the Father of our Lord Jesus Christ, Of whom the whole family in heaven and earth is named.
EPHESIANS 3:14–15

Submitting yourselves one to another in the fear of God. Wives, submit yourselves unto your own husbands, as unto the Lord. For the husband is the head of the wife, even as Christ is the head of the church: and he is the saviour of the body. Therefore as the church is subject unto Christ, so let the wives be to their own husbands in every thing. Husbands, love your wives, even as Christ also loved the church, and gave himself for it; That he might sanctify and cleanse it with the washing of water by the word, That he might present it to himself a glorious church, not having spot, or wrinkle, or any such thing; but that it should be holy and without blemish. So ought men to love their wives as their own bodies. He that loveth his wife loveth himself. For no man ever yet hated his own flesh; but nourisheth and cherisheth it, even as the Lord the church: For we are members of his body, of his flesh, and of his bones. For this cause shall a man leave his father and mother, and shall be joined unto his wife, and they two shall be one flesh. This is a great mystery: but I speak concerning Christ and the church. Nevertheless let every one of you in particular so love his wife even as himself; and the wife see that she reverence her husband.

EPHESIANS 5:21–33

Children, obey your parents in the Lord: for this is right. Honour thy father and mother; which is the first commandment with promise; That it may be well with thee, and thou mayest live long on the earth. And, ye fathers, provoke not your children to wrath: but bring them up in the nurture and admonition of the Lord.

EPHESIANS 6:1–4

Wives, submit yourselves unto your own husbands, as it is fit in the Lord. Husbands, love your wives, and be not bitter against them. Children, obey your parents in all things: for this is well pleasing unto the Lord. Fathers, provoke not your children to anger, lest they be discouraged.

COLOSSIANS 3:18–21

Rejoice with them that do rejoice, and weep with them that weep. Be of the same mind one toward another. Mind not high things, but condescend to men of low estate. Be not wise in your own conceits. Recompense to no man evil for evil. Provide things honest in the sight of all men. If it be possible, as much as lieth in you, live peaceably with all men. Dearly beloved, avenge not yourselves, but rather give place unto wrath: for it is written, Vengeance is mine; I will repay, saith the Lord. Therefore if thine enemy hunger, feed him; if he thirst, give him drink: for in so doing thou shalt heap coals of fire on his head. Be not overcome of evil, but overcome evil with good.

ROMANS 12:15–21

Wherefore comfort yourselves together, and edify one another, even as also ye do.
1 THESSALONIANS 5:11

This is a true saying, if a man desire
the office of a bishop, he desireth a good
work. A bishop then must be blameless,
the husband of one wife, vigilant, sober,
of good behaviour, given to hospitality,
apt to teach; Not given to wine,
no striker, not greedy of filthy lucre;
but patient, not a brawler,
not covetous; One that ruleth well his
own house, having his children in
subjection with all gravity; (For if a
man know not how to rule his own
house, how shall he take care of
the church of God?)
1 Timothy 3:1–5

Let the deacons be the husbands of one wife,
ruling their children and their own houses well.
1 Timothy 3:12

When I call to remembrance the unfeigned
faith that is in thee, which dwelt first in thy
grandmother Lois, and thy mother Eunice; and
I am persuaded that in thee also.
2 Timothy 1:5

Rebuke not an elder, but intreat him as a father; and the younger men as brethren; The elder women as mothers; the younger as sisters, with all purity. Honour widows that are widows indeed. But if any widow have children or nephews, let them learn first to shew piety at home, and to requite their parents: for that is good and acceptable before God. Now she that is a widow indeed, and desolate, trusteth in God, and continueth in supplications and prayers night and day. But she that liveth in pleasure is dead while she liveth. And these things give in charge, that they may be blameless. But if any provide not for his own, and specially for those of his own house, he hath denied the faith, and is worse than an infidel.

1 TIMOTHY 5:1–8

And let us consider one another to provoke unto love and to good works: Not forsaking the assembling of ourselves together, as the manner of some is; but exhorting one another: and so much the more, as ye see the day approaching.

HEBREWS 10:24–25

Likewise, ye wives, be in subjection to your own husbands; that, if any obey not the word, they also may without the word be won by the conversation of the wives; While they behold your chaste conversation coupled with fear. Whose adorning let it not be that outward adorning of plaiting the hair, and of wearing of gold, or of putting on of apparel; But let it be the hidden man of the heart, in that which is not corruptible, even the ornament of a meek and quiet spirit, which is in the sight of God of great price. For after this manner in the old time the holy women also, who trusted in God, adorned themselves, being in subjection unto their own husbands: Even as Sara obeyed Abraham, calling him lord: whose daughters ye are, as long as ye do well, and are not afraid with any amazement. Likewise, ye husbands, dwell with them according to knowledge, giving honour unto the wife, as unto the weaker vessel, and as being heirs together of the grace of life; that your prayers be not hindered. Finally, be ye all of one mind, having compassion one of another, love as brethren, be pitiful, be courteous: Not rendering evil for evil, or railing for railing: but contrariwise blessing; knowing that ye are thereunto called, that ye should inherit a blessing.

1 PETER 3:1–9

And above all things have fervent charity among yourselves: for charity shall cover the multitude of sins. Use hospitality one to another without grudging. As every man hath received the gift, even so minister the same one to another, as good stewards of the manifold grace of God.

1 PETER 4:8–10

The elders which are among you I exhort, who am also an elder, and a witness of the sufferings of Christ, and also a partaker of the glory that shall be revealed: Feed the flock of God which is among you, taking the oversight thereof, not by constraint, but willingly; not for filthy lucre, but of a ready mind; Neither as being lords over God's heritage, but being examples to the flock. And when the chief Shepherd shall appear, ye shall receive a crown of glory that fadeth not away. Likewise, ye younger, submit yourselves unto the elder. Yea, all of you be subject one to another, and be clothed with humility: for God resisteth the proud, and giveth grace to the humble.

1 PETER 5:1–5

Giving

Gifts are one of the best parts of Christmas and are certainly wonderful to receive—but so often the pleasure they bring is fleeting. God's Word promises again and again that giving to others, putting their needs and desires ahead of our own, results in pleasure, joy, and blessing that is lasting. Jesus said, "It is more blessed to give than to receive" (Acts 20:35). Test that promise, and you will find it to be absolutely true.

But thou shalt remember the LORD thy God: for it is he that giveth thee power to get wealth, that he may establish his covenant which he sware unto thy fathers, as it is this day.

DEUTERONOMY 8:18

If there be among you a poor man of one of thy brethren within any of thy gates in thy land which the LORD thy God giveth thee, thou shalt not harden thine heart, nor shut thine hand from thy poor brother: But thou shalt open thine hand wide unto him, and shalt surely lend him sufficient for his need, in that which he wanteth.

DEUTERONOMY 15:7–8

Every man shall give as he is able, according to the blessing of the LORD thy God which he hath given thee.

DEUTERONOMY 16:17

Honour the Lord with thy substance, and with the firstfruits of all thine increase.

PROVERBS 3:9

He that hath pity upon the poor
lendeth unto the Lord; and that which
he hath given will he pay him again.
PROVERBS 19:17

He that giveth unto the poor shall not lack: but
he that hideth his eyes shall have many a curse.
PROVERBS 28:27

Will a man rob God? Yet ye have robbed me.
But ye say, Wherein have we robbed thee? In
tithes and offerings. Ye are cursed with a curse:
for ye have robbed me, even this whole nation.
Bring ye all the tithes into the storehouse, that
there may be meat in mine house, and prove me
now herewith, saith the LORD of hosts, if I will
not open you the windows of heaven, and pour
you out a blessing, that there shall not be room
enough to receive it.

MALACHI 3:8–10

Give to him that asketh thee, and from him that would borrow of thee turn not thou away.

MATTHEW 5:42

Take heed that ye do not your alms before men, to be seen of them: otherwise ye have no reward of your Father which is in heaven. Therefore when thou doest thine alms, do not sound a trumpet before thee, as the hypocrites do in the synagogues and in the streets, that they may have glory of men. Verily I say unto you, They have their reward. But when thou doest alms, let not thy left hand know what thy right hand doeth: That thine alms may be in secret: and thy Father which seeth in secret himself shall reward thee openly.

MATTHEW 6:1–4

Freely ye have received, freely give.

MATTHEW 10:8

Then shall the King say unto them on his right hand, Come, ye blessed of my Father, inherit the kingdom prepared for you from the foundation of the world: For I was an hungred, and ye gave me meat: I was thirsty, and ye gave me drink: I was a stranger, and ye took me in: Naked, and ye clothed me: I was sick, and ye visited me: I was in prison, and ye came unto me. Then shall the righteous answer him, saying, Lord, when saw we thee an hungred, and fed thee? or thirsty, and gave thee drink? When saw we thee a stranger, and took thee in? or naked, and clothed thee? Or when saw we thee sick, or in prison, and came unto thee? And the King shall answer and say unto them, Verily I say unto you, Inasmuch as ye have done it unto one of the least of these my brethren, ye have done it unto me.

MATTHEW 25:34–40

And Jesus sat over against the treasury, and beheld how the people cast money into the treasury: and many that were rich cast in much. And there came a certain poor widow, and she threw in two mites, which make a farthing. And he called unto him his disciples, and saith unto them, Verily I say unto you, That this poor widow hath cast more in, than all they which have cast into the treasury: For all they did cast in of their abundance; but she of her want did cast in all that she had, even all her living.

MARK 12:41–44

He that hath two coats, let him impart to him that hath none; and he that hath meat, let him do likewise.

LUKE 3:11

Give, and it shall be given unto you; good measure, pressed down, and shaken together, and running over, shall men give into your bosom. For with the same measure that ye mete withal it shall be measured to you again.

LUKE 6:38

Sell that ye have, and give alms; provide yourselves bags which wax not old, a treasure in the heavens that faileth not, where no thief approacheth, neither moth corrupteth. For where your treasure is, there will your heart be also.

Luke 12:33–34

And he looked up, and saw the rich men casting their gifts into the treasury. And he saw also a certain poor widow casting in thither two mites. And he said, Of a truth I say unto you, that this poor widow hath cast in more than they all: For all these have of their abundance cast in unto the offerings of God: but she of her penury hath cast in all the living that she had.

Luke 21:1–4

I have shewed you all things, how that so labouring ye ought to support the weak, and to remember the words of the Lord Jesus, how he said, It is more blessed to give than to receive.

Acts 20:35

And though I bestow all my goods to feed the poor, and though I give my body to be burned, and have not charity, it profiteth me nothing.

1 Corinthians 13:3

But this I say, He which soweth sparingly shall reap also sparingly; and he which soweth bountifully shall reap also bountifully. Every man according as he purposeth in his heart, so let him give; not grudgingly, or of necessity: for God loveth a cheerful giver.

2 CORINTHIANS 9:6–7

But if any provide not for his own, and specially for those of his own house, he hath denied the faith, and is worse than an infidel.
1 TIMOTHY 5:8

Charge them that are rich in this world, that they be not highminded, nor trust in uncertain riches, but in the living God, who giveth us richly all things to enjoy; That they do good, that they be rich in good works, ready to distribute, willing to communicate; Laying up in store for themselves a good foundation against the time to come, that they may lay hold on eternal life.

1 TIMOTHY 6:17–19

What doth it profit, my brethren,
though a man say he hath faith,
and have not works? can faith save
him? If a brother or sister be naked,
and destitute of daily food, And one of
you say unto them, Depart in peace,
be ye warmed and filled;
notwithstanding ye give them not
those things which are needful to the
body; what doth it profit? Even so
faith, if it hath not works,
is dead, being alone.

JAMES 2:14–17

Hereby perceive we the love of God, because
he laid down his life for us: and we ought to lay
down our lives for the brethren. But whoso hath
this world's good, and seeth his brother have
need, and shutteth up his bowels of compassion
from him, how dwelleth the love of God in
him? My little children, let us not love in word,
neither in tongue; but in deed and in truth.

1 JOHN 3:16–18

Goodwill

Goodwill is defined with words like *kindness, helpfulness, friendliness, cheerfulness*—qualities that can be hard to find but are very much needed in a hurting, sinful world. Find your goodwill in the promises of God's Word— and then cheerfully share it with others!

The light of the eyes rejoiceth the heart: and a good report maketh the bones fat.

PROVERBS 15:30

A merry heart doeth good like a medicine: but a broken spirit drieth the bones.

PROVERBS 17:22

A man that hath friends must shew himself friendly: and there is a friend that sticketh closer than a brother.

PROVERBS 18:24

For the mountains shall depart, and the hills be removed; but my kindness shall not depart from thee, neither shall the covenant of my peace be removed, saith the LORD that hath mercy on thee.

ISAIAH 54:10

Therefore also now, saith the LORD, turn ye even to me with all your heart, and with fasting, and with weeping, and with mourning: And rend your heart, and not your garments, and turn unto the LORD your God: for he is gracious and merciful, slow to anger, and of great kindness, and repenteth him of the evil.

JOEL 2:12–13

A merry heart maketh a cheerful countenance:
but by sorrow of the heart the spirit is broken.

PROVERBS 15:13

And he prayed unto the LORD, and said, I
pray thee, O LORD, was not this my saying,
when I was yet in my country? Therefore I fled
before unto Tarshish: for I knew that thou art a
gracious God, and merciful, slow to anger, and
of great kindness, and repentest thee of the evil.

JONAH 4:2

*And, behold, they brought to him a
man sick of the palsy, lying on a bed:
and Jesus seeing their faith said unto
the sick of the palsy; Son, be of good
cheer; thy sins be forgiven thee.*

MATTHEW 9:2

But straightway Jesus spake unto them, saying,
Be of good cheer; it is I; be not afraid.

MATTHEW 14:27

For they all saw him, and were troubled. And
immediately he talked with them, and saith
unto them, Be of good cheer: it is I; be not
afraid.

MARK 6:50

And, lo, the angel of the Lord came upon them, and the glory of the Lord shone round about them: and they were sore afraid. And the angel said unto them, Fear not: for, behold, I bring you good tidings of great joy, which shall be to all people. For unto you is born this day in the city of David a Saviour, which is Christ the Lord. And this shall be a sign unto you; Ye shall find the babe wrapped in swaddling clothes, lying in a manger. And suddenly there was with the angel a multitude of the heavenly host praising God, and saying, Glory to God in the highest, and on earth peace, good will toward men.

LUKE 2:9–14

These things I have spoken unto you,
that in me ye might have peace.
In the world ye shall have tribulation:
but be of good cheer;
I have overcome the world.

JOHN 16:33

And the night following the Lord stood by him, and said, Be of good cheer, Paul: for as thou hast testified of me in Jerusalem, so must thou bear witness also at Rome.

ACTS 23:11

And now I exhort you to be of good cheer: for there shall be no loss of any man's life among you, but of the ship. For there stood by me this night the angel of God, whose I am, and whom I serve, Saying, Fear not, Paul; thou must be brought before Caesar: and, lo, God hath given thee all them that sail with thee. Wherefore, sirs, be of good cheer: for I believe God, that it shall be even as it was told me.

ACTS 27:22–25

Having then gifts differing according to the grace that is given to us, whether prophecy, let us prophesy according to the proportion of faith; Or ministry, let us wait on our ministering: or he that teacheth, on teaching; Or he that exhorteth, on exhortation: he that giveth, let him do it with simplicity; he that ruleth, with diligence; he that sheweth mercy, with cheerfulness.

ROMANS 12:6–8

But in all things approving ourselves as the ministers of God, in much patience, in afflictions, in necessities, in distresses, In stripes, in imprisonments, in tumults, in labours, in watchings, in fastings; By pureness, by knowledge, by long suffering, by kindness, by the Holy Ghost, by love unfeigned...

2 Corinthians 6:4–6

Every man according as he purposeth
in his heart, so let him give;
not grudgingly, or of necessity:
for God loveth a cheerful giver.

2 Corinthians 9:7

And hath raised us up together, and made us sit together in heavenly places in Christ Jesus: That in the ages to come he might shew the exceeding riches of his grace in his kindness toward us through Christ Jesus.

Ephesians 2:6–7

Let all bitterness, and wrath, and anger, and clamour, and evil speaking, be put away from you, with all malice: And be ye kind one to another, tenderhearted, forgiving one another, even as God for Christ's sake hath forgiven you.

Ephesians 4:31–32

With good will doing service, as to the Lord, and not to men: Knowing that whatsoever good thing any man doeth, the same shall he receive of the Lord, whether he be bond or free.

EPHESIANS 6:7–8

Some indeed preach Christ even of envy and strife; and some also of good will: The one preach Christ of contention, not sincerely, supposing to add affliction to my bonds: But the other of love, knowing that I am set for the defence of the gospel. What then? notwithstanding, every way, whether in pretence, or in truth, Christ is preached; and I therein do rejoice, yea, and will rejoice.

PHILIPPIANS 1:15–18

Put on therefore, as the elect of God, holy and beloved, bowels of mercies, kindness, humbleness of mind, meekness, longsuffering; Forbearing one another, and forgiving one another, if any man have a quarrel against any: even as Christ forgave you, so also do ye.

COLOSSIANS 3:12–13

But after that the kindness and love of God our Saviour toward man appeared, Not by works of righteousness which we have done, but according to his mercy he saved us, by the washing of regeneration, and renewing of the Holy Ghost; Which he shed on us abundantly through Jesus Christ our Saviour; That being justified by his grace, we should be made heirs according to the hope of eternal life.

TITUS 3:4–7

Use hospitality one to another without grudging. As every man hath received the gift, even so minister the same one to another, as good stewards of the manifold grace of God.

1 PETER 4:9–10

Whereby are given unto us exceeding great and precious promises: that by these ye might be partakers of the divine nature, having escaped the corruption that is in the world through lust. And beside this, giving all diligence, add to your faith virtue; and to virtue knowledge; And to knowledge temperance; and to temperance patience; and to patience godliness; And to godliness brotherly kindness; and to brotherly kindness charity. For if these things be in you, and abound, they make you that ye shall neither be barren nor unfruitful in the knowledge of our Lord Jesus Christ.

2 PETER 1:4–8

The Greatest Gift

Jesus was born as a human baby to live among us and relate to us in every way, but He was also God in human form and perfectly without sin. . .and therefore able to be the sacrifice for all our sin. Our worldly celebrations of Christmastime are festive and fun, but don't let them steal your focus from the real reason to celebrate. Let the promises of God's Word remind you that at Christmas, you are celebrating the greatest gift ever given—our Redeemer, Jesus Christ.

Salvation belongeth unto the LORD: thy
blessing is upon thy people.

PSALM 3:8

Therefore the Lord himself shall give you a sign;
Behold, a virgin shall conceive, and bear a son,
and shall call his name Immanuel.

ISAIAH 7:14

*For unto us a child is born, unto us a
son is given: and the government shall
be upon his shoulder: and his name
shall be called Wonderful, Counsellor,
The mighty God, The everlasting
Father, The Prince of Peace.*

ISAIAH 9:6

But thou, Bethlehem Ephratah, though thou
be little among the thousands of Judah, yet out
of thee shall he come forth unto me that is to
be ruler in Israel; whose goings forth have been
from of old, from everlasting.

MICAH 5:2

And she shall bring forth a son, and thou shalt call his name JESUS: for he shall save his people from their sins. Now all this was done, that it might be fulfilled which was spoken of the Lord by the prophet, saying, Behold, a virgin shall be with child, and shall bring forth a son, and they shall call his name Emmanuel, which being interpreted is, God with us.

MATTHEW 1:21–23

And thou Bethlehem, in the land of Juda, art not the least among the princes of Juda: for out of thee shall come a Governor, that shall rule my people Israel.

MATTHEW 2:6

Behold, thou shalt conceive in thy womb, and bring forth a son, and shalt call his name JESUS. He shall be great, and shall be called the Son of the Highest: and the Lord God shall give unto him the throne of his father David: And he shall reign over the house of Jacob for ever; and of his kingdom there shall be no end.

LUKE 1:31–33

And it came to pass in those days, that there went out a decree from Caesar Augustus that all the world should be taxed. (And this taxing was first made when Cyrenius was governor of Syria.) And all went to be taxed, every one into his own city. And Joseph also went up from Galilee, out of the city of Nazareth, into Judaea, unto the city of David, which is called Bethlehem; (because he was of the house and lineage of David:) To be taxed with Mary his espoused wife, being great with child. And so it was, that, while they were there, the days were accomplished that she should be delivered. And she brought forth her firstborn son, and wrapped him in swaddling clothes, and laid him in a manger; because there was no room for them in the inn. And there were in the same country shepherds abiding in the field, keeping watch over their flock by night. And, lo, the angel of the Lord came upon them, and the glory of the Lord shone round about them: and they were sore afraid.

LUKE 2:1–9

And the angel said unto them, Fear not: for, behold, I bring you good tidings of great joy, which shall be to all people. For unto you is born this day in the city of David a Saviour, which is Christ the Lord. And this shall be a sign unto you; Ye shall find the babe wrapped in swaddling clothes, lying in a manger. And suddenly there was with the angel a multitude of the heavenly host praising God, and saying, Glory to God in the highest, and on earth peace, good will toward men. And it came to pass, as the angels were gone away from them into heaven, the shepherds said one to another, Let us now go even unto Bethlehem, and see this thing which is come to pass, which the Lord hath made known unto us. And they came with haste, and found Mary, and Joseph, and the babe lying in a manger. And when they had seen it, they made known abroad the saying which was told them concerning this child. And all they that heard it wondered at those things which were told them by the shepherds.

LUKE 2:10–18

And, behold, there was a man in Jerusalem, whose name was Simeon; and the same man was just and devout, waiting for the consolation of Israel: and the Holy Ghost was upon him. And it was revealed unto him by the Holy Ghost, that he should not see death, before he had seen the Lord's Christ. And he came by the Spirit into the temple: and when the parents brought in the child Jesus, to do for him after the custom of the law, Then took he him up in his arms, and blessed God, and said, Lord, now lettest thou thy servant depart in peace, according to thy word: For mine eyes have seen thy salvation, Which thou hast prepared before the face of all people; A light to lighten the Gentiles, and the glory of thy people Israel. And Joseph and his mother marvelled at those things which were spoken of him. And Simeon blessed them, and said unto Mary his mother, Behold, this child is set for the fall and rising again of many in Israel; and for a sign which shall be spoken against.

Luke 2:25–34

And there was one Anna, a prophetess, the daughter of Phanuel, of the tribe of Aser: she was of a great age, and had lived with an husband seven years from her virginity; And she was a widow of about fourscore and four years, which departed not from the temple, but served God with fastings and prayers night and day. And she coming in that instant gave thanks likewise unto the Lord, and spake of him to all them that looked for redemption in Jerusalem.

Luke 2:36–38

That whosoever believeth in him should not perish, but have eternal life. For God so loved the world, that he gave his only begotten Son, that whosoever believeth in him should not perish, but have everlasting life. For God sent not his Son into the world to condemn the world; but that the world through him might be saved.

John 3:15–17

There cometh a woman of Samaria to draw water: Jesus saith unto her, Give me to drink. (For his disciples were gone away unto the city to buy meat.) Then saith the woman of Samaria unto him, How is it that thou, being a Jew, askest drink of me, which am a woman of Samaria? for the Jews have no dealings with the Samaritans. Jesus answered and said unto her, If thou knewest the gift of God, and who it is that saith to thee, Give me to drink; thou wouldest have asked of him, and he would have given thee living water. The woman saith unto him, Sir, thou hast nothing to draw with, and the well is deep: from whence then hast thou that living water? Art thou greater than our father Jacob, which gave us the well, and drank thereof himself, and his children, and his cattle? Jesus answered and said unto her, Whosoever drinketh of this water shall thirst again: But whosoever drinketh of the water that I shall give him shall never thirst; but the water that I shall give him shall be in him a well of water springing up into everlasting life.

JOHN 4:7–14

My sheep hear my voice, and I know them, and they follow me: And I give unto them eternal life; and they shall never perish, neither shall any man pluck them out of my hand.

John 10:27–28

Therefore let all the house of Israel know assuredly, that God hath made the same Jesus, whom ye have crucified, both Lord and Christ. Now when they heard this, they were pricked in their heart, and said unto Peter and to the rest of the apostles, Men and brethren, what shall we do? Then Peter said unto them, Repent, and be baptized every one of you in the name of Jesus Christ for the remission of sins, and ye shall receive the gift of the Holy Ghost. For the promise is unto you, and to your children, and to all that are afar off, even as many as the Lord our God shall call.

Acts 2:36–39

But God commendeth his love toward us, in that, while we were yet sinners, Christ died for us. Much more then, being now justified by his blood, we shall be saved from wrath through him.

Romans 5:8–9

For the wages of sin is death;
but the gift of God is eternal life
through Jesus Christ our Lord.

ROMANS 6:23

Wherefore, as by one man sin entered into the
world, and death by sin; and so death passed
upon all men, for that all have sinned: (For
until the law sin was in the world: but sin is
not imputed when there is no law. Nevertheless
death reigned from Adam to Moses, even over
them that had not sinned after the similitude of
Adam's transgression, who is the figure of him
that was to come. But not as the offence, so also
is the free gift. For if through the offence of one
many be dead, much more the grace of God,
and the gift by grace, which is by one man, Jesus
Christ, hath abounded unto many. And not as
it was by one that sinned, so is the gift: for the
judgment was by one to condemnation, but the
free gift is of many offences unto justification.
For if by one man's offence death reigned by
one; much more they which receive abundance
of grace and of the gift of righteousness shall
reign in life by one, Jesus Christ.)

ROMANS 5:12–17

Therefore as by the offence of one judgment came upon all men to condemnation; even so by the righteousness of one the free gift came upon all men unto justification of life. For as by one man's disobedience many were made sinners, so by the obedience of one shall many be made righteous. Moreover the law entered, that the offence might abound. But where sin abounded, grace did much more abound: That as sin hath reigned unto death, even so might grace reign through righteousness unto eternal life by Jesus Christ our Lord.

ROMANS 5:18–21

Thanks be unto God for his unspeakable gift.
2 CORINTHIANS 9:15

That in the ages to come he might shew the exceeding riches of his grace in his kindness toward us through Christ Jesus. For by grace are ye saved through faith; and that not of yourselves: it is the gift of God: Not of works, lest any man should boast.

EPHESIANS 2:7–9

This is a faithful saying, and worthy of all acceptation, that Christ Jesus came into the world to save sinners; of whom I am chief. Howbeit for this cause I obtained mercy, that in me first Jesus Christ might shew forth all longsuffering, for a pattern to them which should hereafter believe on him to life everlasting. Now unto the King eternal, immortal, invisible, the only wise God, be honour and glory for ever and ever. Amen.

1 Timothy 1:15–17

But after that the kindness and love of God our Saviour toward man appeared, Not by works of righteousness which we have done, but according to his mercy he saved us, by the washing of regeneration, and renewing of the Holy Ghost; Which he shed on us abundantly through Jesus Christ our Saviour; That being justified by his grace, we should be made heirs according to the hope of eternal life.

Titus 3:4–7

How shall we escape, if we neglect so great salvation; which at the first began to be spoken by the Lord, and was confirmed unto us by them that heard him; God also bearing them witness, both with signs and wonders, and with divers miracles, and gifts of the Holy Ghost, according to his own will?

HEBREWS 2:3–4

Every good gift and every perfect gift is from above, and cometh down from the Father of lights, with whom is no variableness, neither shadow of turning.

JAMES 1:17

And this is the record, that God hath given to us eternal life, and this life is in his Son.

1 JOHN 5:11

Hope

When Jesus Christ came to earth as a baby, He brought hope to a hurting world. His life and death and resurrection would provide the way for man to reconcile with God and have assurance of an eternal perfect future with Him. Our world says to put our hope in things like wealth and science and other people—but our one true hope is always, ever, only Jesus.

I have set the LORD always before me: because
he is at my right hand, I shall not be moved.
Therefore my heart is glad, and my glory
rejoiceth: my flesh also shall rest in hope.

PSALM 16:8–9

Be of good courage, and he shall strengthen
your heart, all ye that hope in the LORD.

PSALM 31:24

Behold, the eye of the LORD is upon them that
fear him, upon them that hope in his mercy.

PSALM 33:18

For our heart shall rejoice in him, because we
have trusted in his holy name. Let thy mercy, O
LORD, be upon us, according as we hope in thee.

PSALM 33:21–22

For in thee, O LORD, do I hope: thou wilt hear,
O Lord my God.

PSALM 38:15

And now, Lord, what wait I for? my hope is in
thee.

PSALM 39:7

Why art thou cast down, O my soul? and why art thou disquieted in me? hope thou in God: for I shall yet praise him for the help of his countenance.

PSALM 42:5

For thou art my hope, O Lord GOD: thou art my trust from my youth.

PSALM 71:5

But I will hope continually, and will yet praise thee more and more.
PSALM 71:14

That they might set their hope in God, and not forget the works of God, but keep his commandments.

PSALM 78:7

My soul fainteth for thy salvation: but I hope in thy word.

PSALM 119:81

Uphold me according unto thy word, that I may live: and let me not be ashamed of my hope.

PSALM 119:116

The wicked is driven away in his wickedness: but the righteous hath hope in his death.

PROVERBS 14:32

Blessed is the man that trusteth in the Lord, and whose hope the Lord is.

JEREMIAH 17:7

This I recall to my mind, therefore have I hope. It is of the LORD's mercies that we are not consumed, because his compassions fail not. They are new every morning: great is thy faithfulness. The LORD is my portion, saith my soul; therefore will I hope in him.

LAMENTATIONS 3:21–24

It is good that a man should both hope and quietly wait for the salvation of the LORD.

LAMENTATIONS 3:26

The LORD also shall roar out of Zion, and utter his voice from Jerusalem; and the heavens and the earth shall shake: but the LORD will be the hope of his people, and the strength of the children of Israel.

JOEL 3:16

Therefore did my heart rejoice, and my tongue was glad; moreover also my flesh shall rest in hope: Because thou wilt not leave my soul in hell, neither wilt thou suffer thine Holy One to see corruption.

ACTS 2:26–27

And now I stand and am judged for the hope of the promise made of God, unto our fathers.

ACTS 26:6

Therefore being justified by faith, we have peace with God through our Lord Jesus Christ: By whom also we have access by faith into this grace wherein we stand, and rejoice in hope of the glory of God. And not only so, but we glory in tribulations also: knowing that tribulation worketh patience; And patience, experience; and experience, hope: And hope maketh not ashamed; because the love of God is shed abroad in our hearts by the Holy Ghost which is given unto us.

ROMANS 5:1–5

For we are saved by hope: but hope that is seen is not hope: for what a man seeth, why doth he yet hope for? But if we hope for that we see not, then do we with patience wait for it.

ROMANS 8:24–25

Rejoicing in hope; patient in tribulation; continuing instant in prayer.

ROMANS 12:12

For whatsoever things were written aforetime were written for our learning, that we through patience and comfort of the scriptures might have hope.

ROMANS 15:4

Now the God of hope fill you with all joy and peace in believing, that ye may abound in hope, through the power of the Holy Ghost.

ROMANS 15:13

For we stretch not ourselves beyond our measure, as though we reached not unto you: for we are come as far as to you also in preaching the gospel of Christ: Not boasting of things without our measure, that is, of other men's labours; but having hope, when your faith is increased, that we shall be enlarged by you according to our rule abundantly, To preach the gospel in the regions beyond you, and not to boast in another man's line of things made ready to our hand.

2 CORINTHIANS 10:14–16

*For we through the Spirit wait for
the hope of righteousness by faith.*
GALATIANS 5:5

That at that time ye were without Christ, being
aliens from the commonwealth of Israel, and
strangers from the covenants of promise, having
no hope, and without God in the world:
But now in Christ Jesus ye who sometimes were
far off are made nigh by the blood of Christ.
EPHESIANS 2:12–13

Since we heard of your faith in Christ Jesus, and
of the love which ye have to all the saints,
For the hope which is laid up for you in heaven,
whereof ye heard before in the word of the
truth of the gospel; Which is come unto you, as
it is in all the world; and bringeth forth fruit, as
it doth also in you, since the day ye heard of it,
and knew the grace of God in truth.
COLOSSIANS 1:4–6

And you, that were sometime alienated and enemies in your mind by wicked works, yet now hath he reconciled In the body of his flesh through death, to present you holy and unblameable and unreproveable in his sight: If ye continue in the faith grounded and settled, and be not moved away from the hope of the gospel, which ye have heard, and which was preached to every creature which is under heaven; whereof I Paul am made a minister.

COLOSSIANS 1:21–23

To whom God would make known what is the riches of the glory of this mystery among the Gentiles; which is Christ in you, the hope of glory.

COLOSSIANS 1:27

We give thanks to God always for you all, making mention of you in our prayers; Remembering without ceasing your work of faith, and labour of love, and patience of hope in our Lord Jesus Christ, in the sight of God and our Father.

1 THESSALONIANS 1:2–3

Therefore, brethren, stand fast, and hold the traditions which ye have been taught, whether by word, or our epistle. Now our Lord Jesus Christ himself, and God, even our Father, which hath loved us, and hath given us everlasting consolation and good hope through grace, Comfort your hearts, and stablish you in every good word and work.

2 Thessalonians 2:15–17

In hope of eternal life, which God, that cannot lie, promised before the world began.

Titus 1:2

Teaching us that, denying ungodliness and worldly lusts, we should live soberly, righteously, and godly, in this present world; Looking for that blessed hope, and the glorious appearing of the great God and our Saviour Jesus Christ; Who gave himself for us, that he might redeem us from all iniquity, and purify unto himself a peculiar people, zealous of good works.

Titus 2:12–14

That being justified by his grace, we should be made heirs according to the hope of eternal life.

Titus 3:7

And we desire that every one of you do shew
the same diligence to the full assurance of hope
unto the end.

HEBREWS 6:11

Wherein God, willing more abundantly to shew
unto the heirs of promise the immutability
of his counsel, confirmed it by an oath: That
by two immutable things, in which it was
impossible for God to lie, we might have a
strong consolation, who have fled for refuge to
lay hold upon the hope set before us: Which
hope we have as an anchor of the soul, both
sure and stedfast, and which entereth into that
within the veil.

HEBREWS 6:17–19

*For the law made nothing perfect,
but the bringing in of a better
hope did; by the which we
draw nigh unto God.*

HEBREWS 7:19

Blessed be the God and Father of our Lord Jesus
Christ, which according to his abundant mercy
hath begotten us again unto a lively hope by the
resurrection of Jesus Christ from the dead.

1 PETER 1:3

Who verily was foreordained before
the foundation of the world, but was
manifest in these last times for you,
Who by him do believe in God,
that raised him up from the dead,
and gave him glory; that your faith
and hope might be in God.

1 Peter 1:20–21

But sanctify the Lord God in your hearts: and
be ready always to give an answer to every man
that asketh you a reason of the hope that is in
you with meekness and fear.

1 Peter 3:15

And every man that hath this hope in him
purifieth himself, even as he is pure.

1 John 3:3

Joy

The parties, the gifts, the music, the decorations
and lights. . . There's so much joy in the season
of Christmas! Many wonderful things can
bring us happiness here on earth, but not one
of them lasts forever. If we only keep seeking
earthly joys, we will never be fully satisfied.
Knowing Jesus Christ as Savior and finding our
hope and purpose in Him create a joy in us that
can never be diminished, no matter what our
circumstances might be. God's Word points
us again and again to the everlasting joy that is
found in Him alone.

But let all those that put their trust in thee rejoice: let them ever shout for joy, because thou defendest them: let them also that love thy name be joyful in thee. For thou, Lord, wilt bless the righteous; with favour wilt thou compass him as with a shield.

PSALM 5:11–12

Thou wilt shew me the path of life: in thy presence is fulness of joy; at thy right hand there are pleasures for evermore.

PSALM 16:11

Sing unto the Lord, O ye saints of his, and give thanks at the remembrance of his holiness. For his anger endureth but a moment; in his favour is life: weeping may endure for a night, but joy cometh in the morning.

PSALM 30:4–5

Be glad in the Lord, and rejoice, ye righteous: and shout for joy, all ye that are upright in heart.

PSALM 32:11

And my soul shall be joyful in the Lord: it shall rejoice in his salvation.

PSALM 35:9

O let the nations be glad and sing for joy: for thou shalt judge the people righteously, and govern the nations upon earth.

PSALM 67:4

Sing aloud unto God our strength: make a joyful noise unto the God of Jacob.

PSALM 81:1

Justice and judgment are the habitation of thy throne: mercy and truth shall go before thy face. Blessed is the people that know the joyful sound: they shall walk, O LORD, in the light of thy countenance. In thy name shall they rejoice all the day: and in thy righteousness shall they be exalted.

PSALM 89:14–16

O come, let us sing unto the LORD: let us make a joyful noise to the rock of our salvation.
Let us come before his presence with thanksgiving, and make a joyful noise unto him with psalms. For the LORD is a great God, and a great King above all gods.

PSALM 95:1–3

Let the heavens rejoice, and let the earth be glad; let the sea roar, and the fulness thereof. Let the field be joyful, and all that is therein: then shall all the trees of the wood rejoice Before the LORD: for he cometh, for he cometh to judge the earth: he shall judge the world with righteousness, and the people with his truth.

PSALM 96:11–13

O sing unto the LORD a new song; for he hath done marvellous things: his right hand, and his holy arm, hath gotten him the victory. The LORD hath made known his salvation: his righteousness hath he openly shewed in the sight of the heathen. He hath remembered his mercy and his truth toward the house of Israel: all the ends of the earth have seen the salvation of our God. Make a joyful noise unto the LORD, all the earth: make a loud noise, and rejoice, and sing praise. Sing unto the LORD with the harp; with the harp, and the voice of a psalm. With trumpets and sound of cornet make a joyful noise before the LORD, the King. Let the sea roar, and the fulness thereof; the world, and they that dwell therein. Let the floods clap their hands: let the hills be joyful together Before the LORD; for he cometh to judge the earth: with righteousness shall he judge the world, and the people with equity.

PSALM 98

Make a joyful noise unto the LORD, all ye lands.
Serve the LORD with gladness: come before
his presence with singing. Know ye that the
LORD he is God: it is he that hath made us, and
not we ourselves; we are his people, and the
sheep of his pasture. Enter into his gates with
thanksgiving, and into his courts with praise: be
thankful unto him, and bless his name. For the
LORD is good; his mercy is everlasting; and his
truth endureth to all generations.

PSALM 100

*When the Lord turned again the
captivity of Zion, we were like them
that dream. Then was our mouth filled
with laughter, and our tongue with
singing: then said they among the
heathen, The Lord hath done great
things for them. The Lord hath done
great things for us; whereof we are
glad. Turn again our captivity,
O Lord, as the streams in the south.
They that sow in tears shall reap in
joy. He that goeth forth and weepeth,
bearing precious seed, shall doubtless
come again with rejoicing,
bringing his sheaves with him.*

PSALM 126

Praise ye the LORD. Sing unto the LORD a new song, and his praise in the congregation of saints. Let Israel rejoice in him that made him: let the children of Zion be joyful in their King. Let them praise his name in the dance: let them sing praises unto him with the timbrel and harp. For the LORD taketh pleasure in his people: he will beautify the meek with salvation. Let the saints be joyful in glory: let them sing aloud upon their beds.

PSALM 149:1–5

The father of the righteous shall greatly rejoice: and he that begetteth a wise child shall have joy of him. Thy father and thy mother shall be glad, and she that bare thee shall rejoice.

PROVERBS 23:24–25

For God giveth to a man that is good in his sight wisdom, and knowledge, and joy.

ECCLESIASTES 2:26

And in that day thou shalt say, O LORD, I will praise thee: though thou wast angry with me, thine anger is turned away, and thou comfortedst me. Behold, God is my salvation; I will trust, and not be afraid: for the LORD JEHOVAH is my strength and my song; he also is become my salvation. Therefore with joy shall ye draw water out of the wells of salvation. And in that day shall ye say, Praise the LORD, call upon his name, declare his doings among the people, make mention that his name is exalted. Sing unto the LORD; for he hath done excellent things: this is known in all the earth.

ISAIAH 12:1–5

The meek also shall increase their joy in the Lord, and the poor among men shall rejoice in the Holy One of Israel.
ISAIAH 29:19

Sing, O heavens; and be joyful, O earth; and break forth into singing, O mountains: for the LORD hath comforted his people, and will have mercy upon his afflicted.

ISAIAH 49:13

Therefore the redeemed of the LORD shall return, and come with singing unto Zion; and everlasting joy shall be upon their head: they shall obtain gladness and joy; and sorrow and mourning shall flee away.

ISAIAH 51:11

For ye shall go out with joy, and be led forth with peace: the mountains and the hills shall break forth before you into singing, and all the trees of the field shall clap their hands.

ISAIAH 55:12

Even them will I bring to my holy mountain, and make them joyful in my house of prayer: their burnt offerings and their sacrifices shall be accepted upon mine altar; for mine house shall be called an house of prayer for all people.

ISAIAH 56:7

I will greatly rejoice in the LORD, my soul shall be joyful in my God; for he hath clothed me with the garments of salvation, he hath covered me with the robe of righteousness, as a bridegroom decketh himself with ornaments, and as a bride adorneth herself with her jewels.

ISAIAH 61:10

Rejoice ye with Jerusalem, and be glad with her, all ye that love her: rejoice for joy with her, all ye that mourn for her.

ISAIAH 66:10

They departed; and, lo, the star, which they saw in the east, went before them, till it came and stood over where the young child was. When they saw the star, they rejoiced with exceeding great joy.

MATTHEW 2:9–10

His lord said unto him, Well done, thou good and faithful servant: thou hast been faithful over a few things, I will make thee ruler over many things: enter thou into the joy of thy lord.

MATTHEW 25:21

But the angel said unto him, Fear not, Zacharias: for thy prayer is heard; and thy wife Elisabeth shall bear thee a son, and thou shalt call his name John. And thou shalt have joy and gladness; and many shall rejoice at his birth. For he shall be great in the sight of the Lord, and shall drink neither wine nor strong drink; and he shall be filled with the Holy Ghost, even from his mother's womb.

LUKE 1:13–15

And it came to pass, that, when Elisabeth heard
the salutation of Mary, the babe leaped in her
womb; and Elisabeth was filled with the Holy
Ghost: And she spake out with a loud voice,
and said, Blessed art thou among women, and
blessed is the fruit of thy womb. And whence is
this to me, that the mother of my Lord should
come to me? For, lo, as soon as the voice of
thy salutation sounded in mine ears, the babe
leaped in my womb for joy.

LUKE 1:41–44

And Mary said, My soul doth
magnify the Lord, And my spirit
hath rejoiced in God my Saviour.

LUKE 1:46–47

Blessed are ye, when men shall hate you,
and when they shall separate you from their
company, and shall reproach you, and cast out
your name as evil, for the Son of man's sake.
Rejoice ye in that day, and leap for joy: for,
behold, your reward is great in heaven: for
in the like manner did their fathers unto the
prophets.

LUKE 6:22–23

And when he cometh home,
he calleth together his friends
and neighbours, saying unto them,
Rejoice with me; for I have found my
sheep which was lost. I say unto you,
that likewise joy shall be in heaven
over one sinner that repenteth,
more than over ninety and nine just
persons, which need no repentance.

LUKE 15:6–7

And they worshipped him, and returned to
Jerusalem with great joy: And were continually
in the temple, praising and blessing God. Amen.

LUKE 24:52–53

These things have I spoken unto you, that my
joy might remain in you, and that your joy
might be full.

JOHN 15:11

Now Jesus knew that they were desirous to ask him, and said unto them, Do ye enquire among yourselves of that I said, A little while, and ye shall not see me: and again, a little while, and ye shall see me? Verily, verily, I say unto you, That ye shall weep and lament, but the world shall rejoice: and ye shall be sorrowful, but your sorrow shall be turned into joy. A woman when she is in travail hath sorrow, because her hour is come: but as soon as she is delivered of the child, she remembereth no more the anguish, for joy that a man is born into the world. And ye now therefore have sorrow: but I will see you again, and your heart shall rejoice, and your joy no man taketh from you. And in that day ye shall ask me nothing. Verily, verily, I say unto you, Whatsoever ye shall ask the Father in my name, he will give it you. Hitherto have ye asked nothing in my name: ask, and ye shall receive, that your joy may be full.

JOHN 16:19–24

Thou hast made known to me the ways of life; thou shalt make me full of joy with thy countenance.

ACTS 2:28

And the disciples were filled with joy, and with the Holy Ghost.

ACTS 13:52

But none of these things move me, neither count I my life dear unto myself, so that I might finish my course with joy, and the ministry, which I have received of the Lord Jesus, to testify the gospel of the grace of God.

ACTS 20:24

Therefore being justified by faith, we have peace with God through our Lord Jesus Christ: By whom also we have access by faith into this grace wherein we stand, and rejoice in hope of the glory of God.

ROMANS 5:1–2

For if, when we were enemies, we were reconciled to God by the death of his Son, much more, being reconciled, we shall be saved by his life. And not only so, but we also joy in God through our Lord Jesus Christ, by whom we have now received the atonement.

ROMANS 5:10–11

But the fruit of the Spirit is love,
joy, peace, longsuffering, gentleness,
goodness, faith, Meekness, temperance:
against such there is no law.
GALATIANS 5:22–23

Do all things without murmurings and
disputings: That ye may be blameless and
harmless, the sons of God, without rebuke, in
the midst of a crooked and perverse nation,
among whom ye shine as lights in the world;
Holding forth the word of life; that I may
rejoice in the day of Christ, that I have not run
in vain, neither laboured in vain. Yea, and if I
be offered upon the sacrifice and service of your
faith, I joy, and rejoice with you all. For the
same cause also do ye joy, and rejoice with me.
PHILIPPIANS 2:14–18

My brethren, count it all joy when ye fall into
divers temptations; Knowing this, that the
trying of your faith worketh patience. But let
patience have her perfect work, that ye may be
perfect and entire, wanting nothing.
JAMES 1:2–4

Love

The Bible promises us that God is love, and He demonstrated it best by sending His Son as a baby, who would later give up His life in order to save us. Jesus said others will know we are His followers by the way we love each other. At Christmastime especially, when the joy of the season often opens people's hearts, let your love be evident to all, that others might accept Jesus Christ as Savior, too.

Hatred stirreth up strifes: but love covereth all sins.

PROVERBS 10:12

Master, which is the great commandment in the law? Jesus said unto him, Thou shalt love the Lord thy God with all thy heart, and with all thy soul, and with all thy mind. This is the first and great commandment. And the second is like unto it, Thou shalt love thy neighbour as thyself. On these two commandments hang all the law and the prophets.

MATTHEW 22:36–40

And Jesus answered him, The first of all the commandments is, Hear, O Israel; The Lord our God is one Lord: And thou shalt love the Lord thy God with all thy heart, and with all thy soul, and with all thy mind, and with all thy strength: this is the first commandment. And the second is like, namely this, Thou shalt love thy neighbour as thyself. There is none other commandment greater than these.

MARK 12:29–31

And, behold, a certain lawyer stood up, and tempted him, saying, Master, what shall I do to inherit eternal life? He said unto him, What is written in the law? how readest thou? And he answering said, Thou shalt love the Lord thy God with all thy heart, and with all thy soul, and with all thy strength, and with all thy mind; and thy neighbour as thyself.

LUKE 10:25–27

For God so loved the world, that he gave his only begotten Son, that whosoever believeth in him should not perish, but have everlasting life.

JOHN 3:16

A new commandment I give unto you, That ye love one another; as I have loved you, that ye also love one another. By this shall all men know that ye are my disciples, if ye have love one to another.

JOHN 13:34–35

He that hath my commandments, and keepeth them, he it is that loveth me: and he that loveth me shall be loved of my Father, and I will love him, and will manifest myself to him.

JOHN 14:21

Jesus answered and said unto him, If a man love me, he will keep my words: and my Father will love him, and we will come unto him, and make our abode with him. He that loveth me not keepeth not my sayings: and the word which ye hear is not mine, but the Father's which sent me.

John 14:23–24

As the Father hath loved me, so have I loved you: continue ye in my love. If ye keep my commandments, ye shall abide in my love; even as I have kept my Father's commandments, and abide in his love. These things have I spoken unto you, that my joy might remain in you, and that your joy might be full. This is my commandment, That ye love one another, as I have loved you. Greater love hath no man than this, that a man lay down his life for his friends.

John 15:9–13

So when they had dined, Jesus saith to Simon
Peter, Simon, son of Jonas, lovest thou me
more than these? He saith unto him, Yea, Lord;
thou knowest that I love thee. He saith unto
him, Feed my lambs. He saith to him again
the second time, Simon, son of Jonas, lovest
thou me? He saith unto him, Yea, Lord; thou
knowest that I love thee. He saith unto him,
Feed my sheep. He saith unto him the third
time, Simon, son of Jonas, lovest thou me? Peter
was grieved because he said unto him the third
time, Lovest thou me? And he said unto him,
Lord, thou knowest all things; thou knowest
that I love thee. Jesus saith unto him, Feed my
sheep.

JOHN 21:15–17

But God commendeth his love toward us, in that,
while we were yet sinners, Christ died for us.

ROMANS 5:8

For I am persuaded, that neither death, nor life,
nor angels, nor principalities, nor powers, nor
things present, nor things to come, Nor height,
nor depth, nor any other creature, shall be able
to separate us from the love of God, which is in
Christ Jesus our Lord.

ROMANS 8:38–39

*Owe no man any thing, but to love
one another: for he that loveth
another hath fulfilled the law.*

ROMANS 13:8

Though I speak with the tongues of men and
of angels, and have not charity, I am become
as sounding brass, or a tinkling cymbal.
And though I have the gift of prophecy, and
understand all mysteries, and all knowledge; and
though I have all faith, so that I could remove
mountains, and have not charity, I am nothing.
And though I bestow all my goods to feed the
poor, and though I give my body to be burned,
and have not charity, it profiteth me nothing.
Charity suffereth long, and is kind; charity
envieth not; charity vaunteth not itself, is not
puffed up, Doth not behave itself unseemly,
seeketh not her own, is not easily provoked,
thinketh no evil; Rejoiceth not in iniquity,
but rejoiceth in the truth; Beareth all things,
believeth all things, hopeth all things, endureth
all things. Charity never faileth: but whether
there be prophecies, they shall fail; whether
there be tongues, they shall cease; whether there
be knowledge, it shall vanish away.

1 CORINTHIANS 13:1–8

And now abideth faith, hope, charity, these three; but the greatest of these is charity.

1 Corinthians 13:13

Let all your things be done with charity.

1 Corinthians 16:14

And above all these things put on charity, which is the bond of perfectness.

Colossians 3:14

And the Lord make you to increase and abound in love one toward another, and toward all men, even as we do toward you.

1 Thessalonians 3:12

If ye fulfil the royal law according to the scripture, Thou shalt love thy neighbour as thyself, ye do well.

James 2:8

And above all things have fervent charity among yourselves: for charity shall cover the multitude of sins.

1 Peter 4:8

Hereby perceive we the love of God, because he laid down his life for us: and we ought to lay down our lives for the brethren. But whoso hath this world's good, and seeth his brother have need, and shutteth up his bowels of compassion from him, how dwelleth the love of God in him? My little children, let us not love in word, neither in tongue; but in deed and in truth.

1 John 3:16–18

Beloved, let us love one another: for love is of God; and every one that loveth is born of God, and knoweth God. He that loveth not knoweth not God; for God is love. In this was manifested the love of God toward us, because that God sent his only begotten Son into the world, that we might live through him. Herein is love, not that we loved God, but that he loved us, and sent his Son to be the propitiation for our sins. Beloved, if God so loved us, we ought also to love one another. No man hath seen God at any time. If we love one another, God dwelleth in us, and his love is perfected in us.

1 John 4:7–12

And this is love, that we walk after his commandments. This is the commandment, That, as ye have heard from the beginning, ye should walk in it.

2 John 1:6

And we have known and believed the love that God hath to us. God is love; and he that dwelleth in love dwelleth in God, and God in him. Herein is our love made perfect, that we may have boldness in the day of judgment: because as he is, so are we in this world. There is no fear in love; but perfect love casteth out fear: because fear hath torment. He that feareth is not made perfect in love. We love him, because he first loved us. If a man say, I love God, and hateth his brother, he is a liar: for he that loveth not his brother whom he hath seen, how can he love God whom he hath not seen? And this commandment have we from him, That he who loveth God love his brother also.

1 JOHN 4:16–21

Peace

Despite all the uncertainty, disappointment, and heartache we suffer in this life, there is a way to have a true and constant peace in the midst of it. That way is Jesus, trusting that one day He will return and make all things right. At Christmas, celebrate the fact that Jesus came once, and stand firm with peace knowing that He *is* coming back again.

The LORD bless thee, and keep thee: The LORD make his face shine upon thee, and be gracious unto thee: The LORD lift up his countenance upon thee, and give thee peace.

NUMBERS 6:24–26

I will both lay me down in peace, and sleep: for thou, LORD, only makest me dwell in safety.

PSALM 4:8

The LORD will give strength unto his people; the LORD will bless his people with peace.

PSALM 29:11

Depart from evil, and do good; seek peace, and pursue it.

PSALM 34:14

But the meek shall inherit the earth; and shall delight themselves in the abundance of peace.

PSALM 37:11

Evening, and morning, and at noon, will I pray, and cry aloud: and he shall hear my voice. He hath delivered my soul in peace from the battle that was against me: for there were many with me.

PSALM 55:17–18

Pray for the peace of Jerusalem: they shall prosper that love thee. Peace be within thy walls, and prosperity within thy palaces. For my brethren and companions' sakes, I will now say, Peace be within thee. Because of the house of the LORD our God I will seek thy good.

PSALM 122:6–9

My son, forget not my law; but let thine heart keep my commandments: For length of days, and long life, and peace, shall they add to thee. Let not mercy and truth forsake thee: bind them about thy neck; write them upon the table of thine heart: So shalt thou find favour and good understanding in the sight of God and man. Trust in the LORD with all thine heart; and lean not unto thine own understanding. In all thy ways acknowledge him, and he shall direct thy paths.

PROVERBS 3:1–6

When thou liest down, thou shalt not be afraid: yea, thou shalt lie down, and thy sleep shall be sweet.

PROVERBS 3:24

When a man's ways please the LORD, he maketh even his enemies to be at peace with him.

PROVERBS 16:7

For unto us a child is born, unto us a son is given: and the government shall be upon his shoulder: and his name shall be called Wonderful, Counsellor, The mighty God, The everlasting Father, The Prince of Peace. Of the increase of his government and peace there shall be no end, upon the throne of David, and upon his kingdom, to order it, and to establish it with judgment and with justice from henceforth even for ever.

Isaiah 9:6–7

Thou wilt keep him in perfect peace, whose mind is stayed on thee: because he trusteth in thee. Trust ye in the Lord for ever: for in the Lord Jehovah is everlasting strength.

Isaiah 26:3–4

Lord, thou wilt ordain peace for us: for thou also hast wrought all our works in us.

Isaiah 26:12

And the work of righteousness shall be peace; and the effect of righteousness quietness and assurance for ever. And my people shall dwell in a peaceable habitation, and in sure dwellings, and in quiet resting places.

Isaiah 32:17–18

Fear thou not; for I am with thee: be not dismayed; for I am thy God: I will strengthen thee; yea, I will help thee; yea, I will uphold thee with the right hand of my righteousness.

ISAIAH 41:10

O that thou hadst hearkened to my commandments! then had thy peace been as a river, and thy righteousness as the waves of the sea.

ISAIAH 48:18

For thus saith the LORD, That after seventy years be accomplished at Babylon I will visit you, and perform my good word toward you, in causing you to return to this place. For I know the thoughts that I think toward you, saith the LORD, thoughts of peace, and not of evil, to give you an expected end. Then shall ye call upon me, and ye shall go and pray unto me, and I will hearken unto you.

JEREMIAH 29:10–12

Behold, I will bring it health and cure, and I will cure them, and will reveal unto them the abundance of peace and truth.

JEREMIAH 33:6

Therefore I say unto you, Take no thought for your life, what ye shall eat, or what ye shall drink; nor yet for your body, what ye shall put on. Is not the life more than meat, and the body than raiment? Behold the fowls of the air: for they sow not, neither do they reap, nor gather into barns; yet your heavenly Father feedeth them. Are ye not much better than they? Which of you by taking thought can add one cubit unto his stature? And why take ye thought for raiment? Consider the lilies of the field, how they grow; they toil not, neither do they spin: And yet I say unto you, That even Solomon in all his glory was not arrayed like one of these. Wherefore, if God so clothe the grass of the field, which to day is, and to morrow is cast into the oven, shall he not much more clothe you, O ye of little faith? Therefore take no thought, saying, What shall we eat? or, What shall we drink? or, Wherewithal shall we be clothed? (For after all these things do the Gentiles seek:) for your heavenly Father knoweth that ye have need of all these things. But seek ye first the kingdom of God, and his righteousness; and all these things shall be added unto you. Take therefore no thought for the morrow: for the morrow shall take thought for the things of itself. Sufficient unto the day is the evil thereof.

MATTHEW 6:25–34

And he was in the hinder part of the ship, asleep on a pillow: and they awake him, and say unto him, Master, carest thou not that we perish? And he arose, and rebuked the wind, and said unto the sea, Peace, be still. And the wind ceased, and there was a great calm. And he said unto them, Why are ye so fearful? how is it that ye have no faith?

MARK 4:38–40

For every one shall be salted with fire, and every sacrifice shall be salted with salt. Salt is good: but if the salt have lost his saltness, wherewith will ye season it? Have salt in yourselves, and have peace one with another.

MARK 9:49–50

Glory to God in the highest, and on earth peace, good will toward men.
LUKE 2:14

Peace I leave with you, my peace I give unto you: not as the world giveth, give I unto you. Let not your heart be troubled, neither let it be afraid.
JOHN 14:27

These things I have spoken unto you, that in me ye might have peace. In the world ye shall have tribulation: but be of good cheer; I have overcome the world.

JOHN 16:33

To all that be in Rome, beloved of God, called to be saints: Grace to you and peace from God our Father, and the Lord Jesus Christ.

ROMANS 1:7

Tribulation and anguish, upon every soul of man that doeth evil, of the Jew first, and also of the Gentile; But glory, honour, and peace, to every man that worketh good, to the Jew first, and also to the Gentile.

ROMANS 2:9–10

Therefore being justified by faith, we have peace with God through our Lord Jesus Christ.

ROMANS 5:1

For to be carnally minded is death; but to be spiritually minded is life and peace.

ROMANS 8:6

And the God of peace shall bruise Satan under your feet shortly. The grace of our Lord Jesus Christ be with you.

ROMANS 16:20

For the unbelieving husband is sanctified by the wife, and the unbelieving wife is sanctified by the husband: else were your children unclean; but now are they holy. But if the unbelieving depart, let him depart. A brother or a sister is not under bondage in such cases: but God hath called us to peace. For what knowest thou, O wife, whether thou shalt save thy husband? or how knowest thou, O man, whether thou shalt save thy wife?

1 CORINTHIANS 7:14–16

Finally, brethren, farewell. Be perfect, be of good comfort, be of one mind, live in peace; and the God of love and peace shall be with you.

2 CORINTHIANS 13:11

But the fruit of the Spirit is love, joy, peace, longsuffering, gentleness, goodness, faith, Meekness, temperance: against such there is no law.

GALATIANS 5:22–23

But now in Christ Jesus ye who sometimes were far off are made nigh by the blood of Christ. For he is our peace, who hath made both one, and hath broken down the middle wall of partition between us; Having abolished in his flesh the enmity, even the law of commandments contained in ordinances; for to make in himself of twain one new man, so making peace; And that he might reconcile both unto God in one body by the cross, having slain the enmity thereby: And came and preached peace to you which were afar off, and to them that were nigh. For through him we both have access by one Spirit unto the Father.

EPHESIANS 2:13–18

I therefore, the prisoner of the Lord, beseech you that ye walk worthy of the vocation wherewith ye are called, With all lowliness and meekness, with longsuffering, forbearing one another in love; Endeavouring to keep the unity of the Spirit in the bond of peace.

EPHESIANS 4:1–3

Peace be to the brethren, and love with faith,
from God the Father and the Lord Jesus Christ.

EPHESIANS 6:23

Be careful for nothing; but in every thing by
prayer and supplication with thanksgiving
let your requests be made known unto God.
And the peace of God, which passeth all
understanding, shall keep your hearts and
minds through Christ Jesus.

PHILIPPIANS 4:6–7

And let the peace of God rule in your hearts, to
the which also ye are called in one body; and be
ye thankful.

COLOSSIANS 3:15

Flee also youthful lusts: but follow
righteousness, faith, charity, peace, with them
that call on the Lord out of a pure heart.

2 TIMOTHY 2:22

Follow peace with all men, and holiness,
without which no man shall see the Lord.

HEBREWS 12:14

For he that will love life, and see good days, let
him refrain his tongue from evil, and his lips
that they speak no guile: Let him eschew evil,
and do good; let him seek peace, and ensue it.

1 Peter 3:10–11

Humble yourselves therefore under the mighty
hand of God, that he may exalt you in due time:
Casting all your care upon him; for he careth
for you.

1 Peter 5:6–7

*Wherefore, beloved, seeing that ye
look for such things, be diligent that
ye may be found of him in peace,
without spot, and blameless.*

2 Peter 3:14

Grace be with you, mercy, and peace, from God
the Father, and from the Lord Jesus Christ, the
Son of the Father, in truth and love.

2 John 1:3

Mercy unto you, and peace, and love,
be multiplied.

Jude 1:2

Serving Others

Jesus demonstrated repeatedly how He came to serve others, and He ultimately gave up His very life for us. As His followers, we are called to the same demonstrations of love, putting others before ourselves, imitating the love of Jesus, and pointing others to Him. At Christmastime especially, open up your arms and your hands and all your resources to embrace those around you and help take care of their needs—just like Jesus would do.

And whosoever will be chief among you, let him be your servant: Even as the Son of man came not to be ministered unto, but to minister, and to give his life a ransom for many.

MATTHEW 20:27–28

Then shall the King say unto them on his right hand, Come, ye blessed of my Father, inherit the kingdom prepared for you from the foundation of the world: For I was an hungred, and ye gave me meat: I was thirsty, and ye gave me drink: I was a stranger, and ye took me in: Naked, and ye clothed me: I was sick, and ye visited me: I was in prison, and ye came unto me. Then shall the righteous answer him, saying, Lord, when saw we thee an hungred, and fed thee? or thirsty, and gave thee drink? When saw we thee a stranger, and took thee in? or naked, and clothed thee? Or when saw we thee sick, or in prison, and came unto thee? And the King shall answer and say unto them, Verily I say unto you, Inasmuch as ye have done it unto one of the least of these my brethren, ye have done it unto me.

MATTHEW 25:34–40

So after he had washed their feet, and had taken his garments, and was set down again, he said unto them, Know ye what I have done to you? Ye call me Master and Lord: and ye say well; for so I am. If I then, your Lord and Master, have washed your feet; ye also ought to wash one another's feet.

JOHN 13:12–14

Take heed therefore unto yourselves, and to all the flock, over the which the Holy Ghost hath made you overseers, to feed the church of God, which he hath purchased with his own blood.

ACTS 20:28

For though I be free from all men, yet have I made myself servant unto all, that I might gain the more.
1 CORINTHIANS 9:19

And let us not be weary in well doing: for in due season we shall reap, if we faint not. As we have therefore opportunity, let us do good unto all men, especially unto them who are of the household of faith.

GALATIANS 6:9–10

What doth it profit, my brethren, though a man say he hath faith, and have not works? can faith save him? If a brother or sister be naked, and destitute of daily food, And one of you say unto them, Depart in peace, be ye warmed and filled; notwithstanding ye give them not those things which are needful to the body; what doth it profit? Even so faith, if it hath not works, is dead, being alone. Yea, a man may say, Thou hast faith, and I have works: shew me thy faith without thy works, and I will shew thee my faith by my works.

JAMES 2:14–18

Use hospitality one to another without grudging. As every man hath received the gift, even so minister the same one to another, as good stewards of the manifold grace of God.
1 PETER 4:9–10

Hereby perceive we the love of God, because he laid down his life for us: and we ought to lay down our lives for the brethren. But whoso hath this world's good, and seeth his brother have need, and shutteth up his bowels of compassion from him, how dwelleth the love of God in him? My little children, let us not love in word, neither in tongue; but in deed and in truth.
1 JOHN 3:16–18

Thankfulness

No matter what your Christmas plans or budget, let the promises of God's Word encourage you in all you've been given, and choose each day—each *moment*, if necessary— to focus on the blessings in your own life. Don't compare with others. Be thankful for what *you* have been given! A heart that is full of gratitude toward God for all He does and all He is going to do is a truly happy heart.

Give thanks unto the LORD, call upon his name, make known his deeds among the people.

1 CHRONICLES 16:8

O give thanks unto the Lord; for he is good; for his mercy endureth for ever.

1 CHRONICLES 16:34

I will extol thee, O LORD; for thou hast lifted me up, and hast not made my foes to rejoice over me. O LORD my God, I cried unto thee, and thou hast healed me. O LORD, thou hast brought up my soul from the grave: thou hast kept me alive, that I should not go down to the pit. Sing unto the LORD, O ye saints of his, and give thanks at the remembrance of his holiness. For his anger endureth but a moment; in his favour is life: weeping may endure for a night, but joy cometh in the morning.

PSALM 30:1–5

Offer unto God thanksgiving; and pay thy vows unto the most High: And call upon me in the day of trouble: I will deliver thee, and thou shalt glorify me.

PSALM 50:14–15

Make a joyful noise unto the LORD, all ye lands. Serve the LORD with gladness: come before his presence with singing. Know ye that the LORD he is God: it is he that hath made us, and not we ourselves; we are his people, and the sheep of his pasture. Enter into his gates with thanksgiving, and into his courts with praise: be thankful unto him, and bless his name. For the LORD is good; his mercy is everlasting; and his truth endureth to all generations.

PSALM 100:1–5

O give thanks unto the LORD; call upon his name: make known his deeds among the people. Sing unto him, sing psalms unto him: talk ye of all his wondrous works. Glory ye in his holy name: let the heart of them rejoice that seek the LORD. Seek the LORD, and his strength: seek his face evermore. Remember his marvellous works that he hath done; his wonders, and the judgments of his mouth.

PSALM 105:1–5

*Thanks be unto God for
his unspeakable gift.*
2 CORINTHIANS 9:15

Speaking to yourselves in psalms and hymns and spiritual songs, singing and making melody in your heart to the Lord; Giving thanks always for all things unto God and the Father in the name of our Lord Jesus Christ.

EPHESIANS 5:19–20

Be careful for nothing; but in every thing by prayer and supplication with thanksgiving let your requests be made known unto God.

PHILIPPIANS 4:6

And let the peace of God rule in your hearts, to the which also ye are called in one body; and be ye thankful.

COLOSSIANS 3:15

And whatsoever ye do in word or deed, do all in the name of the Lord Jesus, giving thanks to God and the Father by him.

COLOSSIANS 3:17

In every thing give thanks: for this is the will of God in Christ Jesus concerning you.

1 THESSALONIANS 5:18